Getting into
Medical School

D1350878

2014 entry

Getting into guides

Getting into

Medical School

2014 entry

Simon Horner

18th edition

trotman | **t**

Getting into Medical School

This 18th edition published in 2013 by Trotman Publishing, an imprint of Crimson Publishing, Westminster House, Kew Road, Richmond, Surrey TW9 2ND

© Joe Ruston 1996; Joe Ruston and James Burnett 1998, 2000, 2001, 2002, 2003, 2004, 2005, 2006; James Burnett 2007, 2008; Steven Piumatti 2009, 2010; Simon Horner and Steven Piumatti 2011; Simon Horner 2012, 2013

Previously published by Trotman & Co Ltd

Author: Simon Horner

British Library Cataloguing in Publication Data
A catalogue record for this book is available from the British Library

ISBN 978 1 90604 194 6

Typeset by IDSUK (DataConnection) Ltd
Printed and bound by TJ International Ltd, Padstow, Cornwall

Contents

Contents

About the author

Simon Horner is Head of Science at Mander Portman Woodward in London and runs the college's medical programme.

Acknowledgements

In order to write this book, I have needed help from many sources. Without the help of the medical schools' admissions departments, this book would not exist, and I would like to record my gratitude to all of the people who gave up their time to answer my questions. I am very grateful to James Barton in particular for his help. Also to Jo Carter for her administrative help in collecting data. Finally, I would like to thank the students who have provided me with interview questions, factual material and encouragement.

Simon Horner
November 2012

About this book

First of all, a note on terminology. Throughout this guide, the term 'medical school' includes the university departments of medicine. Second, entry requirements have been quoted in AS and A level terms; a general guide to the grades or scores that you need if you are taking Scottish Highers, the International Baccalaureate or other qualifications can be found on page 2.

This book is divided into nine main chapters, which aim to cover three major obstacles that would-be doctors may face:

- getting an interview at medical school
- getting a conditional offer
- getting the right A level grades.

The nine chapters discuss the following:

1. the study of medicine
2. the application process and getting an interview
3. the interview process
4. current issues that may come up at interview
5. results day
6. non-standard applications
7. fees and funding
8. careers opportunities
9. further information.

Chapter 1 gives information on the actual study of medicine, different teaching styles and postgraduate study as well as possible specialisations and post-degree course options.

Chapter 2 deals with the preparation that you will need to undertake in order to make your application as irresistible as possible to get an offer and/or an interview. It includes advice on work experience, how to choose a medical school, sample questions from admissions tests such as UKCAT and BMAT and the mechanics of the UCAS application process.

Chapter 3 provides advice on what to expect at the interview stage, current topics, issues you may be questioned on and how to ensure that you come across as a potential doctor.

Chapter 4 presents some key information on contemporary and topical medical issues, such as the structure of the NHS, world health and statistics on some of the most well-known diseases and illnesses.

Knowing about medical issues is a must, particularly if you are called in for an interview.

Chapter 5 looks at the options that you have at your disposal on results day and describes the steps that you need to take if you are holding an offer or if you have been unsuccessful and have not been given an offer.

Chapter 6 is aimed primarily at overseas students and any other 'non-standard' applicants – mature students, graduates, students who have studied arts A levels and retake students (most medical schools consider non-standard applicants). The chapter also includes some advice for those who want to study medicine outside the UK, say, for example, in the US.

Chapter 7 gives some useful information regarding fees and funding for medical students, as well as bursaries and scholarships that are available, while **Chapter 8** looks at career options in medicine.

Finally, in **Chapter 9**, further information is given in terms of courses and further reading. A number of other excellent books are available on the subject of getting into medical school. The contact details of the various medical groups and universities can also be found here. After Chapter 9 a **glossary** can be found of many of the terms used throughout the book.

The difference between other guides on getting into medical school and this one is that this guide is a route map; it tells you the path to follow if you want to be a doctor. Because of this, it is rather bossy and dictatorial. I make no apology for this, because I have seen far too many aspiring medical students who took the wrong subjects, who didn't bother to find work experience and who never asked themselves why they wanted to be a doctor before their interviews. Their path into medicine was made unnecessarily difficult because they didn't prepare properly.

Throughout the book you will find case studies and examples of material that will reflect to some extent the theme being discussed at that point. I hope that you find these real-life examples illuminating.

Finally, the views expressed in this book, though informed by conversations with staff at medical schools and elsewhere, are my own, unless specifically attributed to a contributor in the text.

Introduction

A realistic chance

Only around 40% of applicants for medicine are successful in gaining places. Does this mean that the remaining 60% were unsuitable? The answer, of course, is no. Many of those who are rejected are extremely strong candidates, with high grades at GCSE and AS under their belts and the personalities and qualities that would make them into excellent doctors. There are a fixed number of medical school places available each year and so not all candidates can be successful. But many promising applicants do not put themselves in a position whereby they can be given proper consideration, simply because they do not prepare thoroughly enough.

Ideally, your preparation should begin at least two years before you submit your application, but if you have come to the decision to apply to study medicine more recently, or if you were unaware of what steps you need to take in order to prepare a strong application, don't worry. It is not too late. Even over a relatively short period of time (a few months) you can put together a convincing application.

According to the latest available statistics from UCAS on entries and applicants for the 2012 application cycle intake into medical schools, there was a further small increase in applicants compared with the 2011 numbers. By the October deadline, UCAS had received around 17,000 applications for medical school places from UK students and a further 4,700 applications from international students. Therefore, in 2012, around 21,726 students were battling for the approximately 8,000 places that are available at UK medical schools. There were 379 Clearing accepts.

UK students were more successful in gaining places (40% of applicants gained places) than international students, of whom only about one in four was successful. Female applicants outnumbered male applicants – 55% of all applicants were female – but the success rates of each sex were comparable.

Table 1 gives some comparisons and data on the 2011 application cycle.

Table 1 Number of applicants in 2012

Type of applicant	Number of applicants	Applicants accepted onto degree courses	Successful applicants (%)
UK	16,366	7,007	42.81%
EU	1,907	193	10.12%
Non-EU	2,931	605	20.64%
Male	9,470	3,647	38.51%
Female	11,734	4,158	35.44%
Total	21,204	7,805	36.81%

Reproduced with kind permission of UCAS.

The grades you need

Table 10 (see pages 152–154) shows that, with a few exceptions, the A level grades you need for medicine are AAA. You might be lucky and get an offer of AAB, but you won't know that until six months before the exams, so you can't rely on it. Some medical schools, such as Cambridge and Brighton and Sussex, may now ask for an A* grade for 2014 entry.

As a general guide, candidates with qualifications other than A levels are likely to need the following:

- Scottish: AAAAB in Highers or AA in Advanced Highers to include AAAAB in Highers
- International Baccalaureate: around 36–38 points, including 6, 6, 6 at Higher level (including chemistry)
- European Baccalaureate: roughly 80% overall, with at least 80% in chemistry and another full option science/mathematical subject.

But there's more to it than grades . . .

If getting a place to study medicine was purely a matter of achieving the right grades, medical schools would demand A*AA at A level (or equivalent) and 10 A* grades at GCSE, and they would not bother to interview. However, to become a successful doctor requires many skills, academic and otherwise, and it is the job of the admissions staff to try to identify who of the thousands of applicants are the most suitable. It would be misleading to say that anyone, with enough effort, could become a doctor, but it is important for candidates who have the potential to succeed to make the best use of their applications.

Non-standard and second-time applications

Not all successful applicants apply during their final year of A levels. Some have retaken their exams, while others have used a gap year to add substance to their UCAS application. Again, it would be wrong to say that anyone who reapplies will automatically get a place, but good candidates should not assume that rejection first time round means the end of their medical career aspirations.

Gaining a place as a retake student or as a second-time applicant is not as easy as it used to be, but candidates who can demonstrate genuine commitment alongside the right personal and academic qualities still have a good chance of success if they go about their applications in the right way. The admissions staff at the medical schools tend to be extremely helpful and, except at the busiest times of the year when they simply do not have the time, they will give advice and encouragement to suitable applicants.

Admissions

The medical schools make strenuous efforts to maintain fair selection procedures: UCAS applications are generally seen by more than one selector, interview panels are given strict guidelines about what they can (and cannot) ask, and most make detailed statistics available about the backgrounds of the students they interview. Above all, admissions staff will tell you that they are looking for good 'all-rounders' who can communicate effectively with others, are academically able and are genuinely enthusiastic about medicine – if you think that this sounds like you, then read on!

Reflections of a doctor

The words below from a qualified practitioner and then from a mature student embarking on a career in medicine express and reflect some of the many challenges and rewards that you may also face in your own journey to become a doctor. Like every journey, the grandest ones start with the first minuscule step.

There is a true joy in qualifying as a doctor. All of the hurdles of getting into medical school and the midnight oil burnt to pass the countless exams are behind you, and for the first time in your life you have the honour of putting the initials 'Dr' in front of your name. It's better than being knighted.

However, your journey through medicine is only just beginning. Ahead of you lie more hurdles and the difficult choices of what field to specialise in.

Anyone considering medicine will understand the rewards of medicine: the privilege of caring for others and being let in to their most private world; the opportunity to be an advocate for the most vulnerable in society; the respect that comes from being in the most trusted profession; the variety of work; the intellectual challenge; and the chance to work in a team of like-minded individuals.

There are many challenges as well. All new doctors will need to sub-specialise, and that requires more exams. Gaining the experience to become a good doctor requires putting in the hours, day and night. Expectations are ever higher and consumer demands can lead to difficult consultations and litigation. While making people better can be heart-warming, making mistakes or seeing people become sicker and die can be heart-wrenching.

One of the early decisions to make is whether to become a general practitioner or a hospital doctor. The first phase in your career is to gather all the knowledge and skills required to become certified in your chosen area. The second is to build on your experience and confidence, and often to sub-specialise in discrete clinical areas. The third stage is to act as a mentor and leader of more junior colleagues. All three stages provide the chance to develop interests in education, research or medical management.

Medicine is a broad church that accommodates varied brethren, from the compassionate to the technical, the intellectual to the practical. There is one theme that is common to all: the desire to improve the well-being of individuals and communities.

While the work can be stressful, and the responsibility can sometimes be crushing, being a doctor will always be occupying and fulfilling.

Dr John Wright
Director of Clinical Governance and
Operations Medical Director at Bradford Royal Infirmary

Emma is a history graduate who studied A level biology and chemistry over one year. She received one offer and achieved two A* grades in the June examinations.

Graduate-entry medicine is an enormous step up. Rather than just being theoretical, it is an accurate reflection of the profession. The demands on you are enormous and the stress that goes with it is not to be taken lightly. I now completely understand the importance of it.

The best advice that I can give you is to ask questions; however, not just to ask but to listen to the answers you are given. It is about how you use what you are told to its best advantage. Work experience is of paramount importance. Yes, it is a requirement for the course. However, more than that it helps to confirm that this is the correct way forward. There is no glamour to wanting to be a doctor. You have to be prepared for the trauma and bodily fluids that you will inevitably encounter. Far better to experience those on work experience so that you have an accurate idea rather than later when working within the profession itself.

I had a lot of advice from admissions tutors when I applied and I cannot thank them enough for it. They were always there to clarify specifics for me. That said, do not ask them questions that you can find out for yourself in their literature. You should only ask specific questions on the course or the teaching methods that you require clarification on in order to make a decision as to which university to apply to. Remember, they want your business so they are happy to answer questions.

If you want to be a doctor, it has to be your burning ambition. Go into it for the right reasons. You are responsible for the welfare of others and that is a position of great responsibility.

1 | Studying medicine

This chapter mainly discusses studying medicine as an undergraduate course. For information on postgraduate courses, see the section entitled 'Postgraduate courses' on page 16.

Medical courses are carefully planned by the General Medical Council (GMC) to give students a wide range of academic and practical experience, which will lead to final qualification as a doctor. The main difference between medical schools is the method of teaching. At the end of the five-year course, students will – if they have met the high academic standards demanded – be awarded a Bachelor of Medicine or Bachelor of Medicine and Surgery (referred to as an MB or an MBBS respectively). Many doctors come out with an MBChB – it all depends on which medical school you go to. Like dentistry, the ChB, i.e. Honours, is largely an honorary title. The MB is the Bachelor of Medicine while the ChB is the Bachelor of Surgery from the Latin *Baccalaureus Chirurgiae*.

It is well worth noting that, at this stage, doctors are graduates and have yet to do (if they so wish) a postgraduate doctoral degree such as a PhD. So they are, in the academic and philosophic sense, not doctors. However, when doctors specialise, it is then necessary to have a post-doctoral degree.

Teaching styles

The structure of all medical courses is similar, with most institutions offering two years of pre-clinical studies (often undertaken with dentistry students at the same university) followed by three years of clinical studies. However, schools differ in the ways in which they deliver the material, so it is very important to get hold of, and thoroughly read, the latest prospectuses of each university to which you are thinking of applying.

Medical courses can be classified as either traditional or problem-based learning (PBL) or lecture/teaching-based. In addition, the style of teaching can be integrated.

The table below shows a list of the medical schools in the UK along with the teaching style they practise.

Table 2: Teaching styles

Medical school	Teaching style
Aberdeen	Traditional
Cambridge	Traditional
Oxford	Traditional
Queen's University Belfast	Traditional
St Andrews	Traditional/Integrated
Glasgow	PBL
Peninsula	PBL
Liverpool	PBL
Manchester	PBL
Keele University	PBL
Barts and The London	Integrated/PBL
University of East Anglia	Integrated/PBL
Hull York	Integrated/PBL
Edinburgh	Integrated
Imperial College	Integrated
King's	Integrated
Leeds	Integrated
Leicester	Integrated
Newcastle	Integrated
Nottingham and Derby	Integrated
Royal Free and University College London	Integrated
St George's Hospital	Integrated
Sheffield	Integrated
Southampton	Integrated
Warwick	Integrated

Traditional courses

This is the more long-established lecture-based style, using didactic methods. The majority of these courses are subject-based ones, where lectures are the most appropriate way of delivering the information. It has to be said that these courses are a rarity today and are perhaps limited to establishments such as Oxford, Cambridge and St Andrews, where there is a definite pre-clinical/clinical divide and the pre-clinical years are taught very rigidly in subjects.

TIP!

Find out more details about these traditional-based learning courses by going to the websites for the following medical schools:

- University of Cambridge: www.medschl.cam.ac.uk
- University of Oxford: www.medsci.ox.ac.uk
- University of St Andrews: medicine.st-andrews.ac.uk.

Problem-based learning (PBL)

The PBL course, which has been commended by the GMC, was pioneered by medical schools such as Liverpool and Manchester and subsequently taken up by a number of other medical schools such as Barts and The London, East Anglia, Hull York, Keele, Peninsula and Sheffield. The course is taught with a patient-oriented approach. From year 1 onwards, students are heavily involved in clinical scenarios, with the focus on the student to demonstrate self-motivation and proactive self-directed learning. This type of teaching/learning is designed to get away from the previous traditional 'spoon-fed' approach; therefore, those who are used to the spoon feeding of information may take some time to adjust.

Course structure: Barts and The London, 2012 (PBL)

The programme has been designed to provide students with the medical knowledge, clinical skills and professional attitude that are required to become a competent and safe Foundation Year (FY1) doctor. The curriculum closely follows the recommendations set out in *Tomorrow's Doctors* (General Medical Council, September 2009).

The curriculum

The curriculum is taught in a series of modules that are based on body systems, which, in turn, encompass various scientific and medical themes. These systems and themes are shown in the table below.

Table 3 Body system details

System	Details
The whole person	The healthy person, emergency, acute and chronic care
Cardiorespiratory	Cardiovascular, respiratory medicine, haematology
Human development	Child health, obstetrics and gynaecology
Metabolism	Endocrine, renal, gastrointestinal
Brain and behaviour	Psychiatry, neuroscience, ophthalmology
Locomotor	Musculoskeletal, dermatology, healthcare of the elderly

Each system is visited a minimum of three times during the programme. Teaching within the systems is based on three themes:

1. the doctor as a scholar
2. the doctor as a practitioner
3. the doctor as a professional.

Timetable

The MBBS programme is divided into three phases.

Table 4 The MBBS programme phases

Phase	5-year programme UCAS code: A100	4-year graduate entry programme UCAS code: A101
1	Years 1 and 2	Year 1
2	Years 3 and 4	Years 2 and 3
3	Year 5 (final)	Year 4 (final)

Phase 1

Phase 1 is taught via a series of systems-based modules which introduce the basic biological sciences and address key topics including normal biological structure and function of cells, organs and body systems; the effect of illness on people and their families; and the impact of environmental and social factors on health.

Students take five systems-based modules and three student-selected components (SSCs) each year.

GEP students

Students take eight modules: six systems-based plus human sciences and public health and infection and immunity.

In addition, GEP (Graduate Entry Programme) students take an introduction to inter-professional learning (IPE); this covers the core knowledge, skills and capabilities that are common to all healthcare professions and includes subjects such as ethics and law and clinical and communication studies. GEP students do not complete an SSC programme in their first year.

Students form an effective and mutually supportive community that encourages collaborative learning through a programme of PBL scenarios, which involve groups of 8–10 students and a facilitator working together to tackle a problem presented as a clinical scenario. In addition, learning is facilitated by a programme of didactic lectures, workshops and other group activities. Regular patient contact is a key feature of these early years.

Phase 2

During phase 2, students regularly return to the medical school for teaching weeks and assessments as well as being introduced to clinical medicine through a series of placements in our associate teaching hospitals. Students may visit a variety of hospitals during their clinical years. Their knowledge and clinical skills are enhanced by working alongside clinical teams both in the hospital and also within community placements.

All students complete three SSCs a year; these are based around clinical scenarios, patient interviews and history taking and associated issues surrounding their chosen patient.

Phase 3

The final year of the programme provides students with clinical and community placements, practical skills and first-hand experience of the working life of a first-year Foundation Year (FY1) doctor.

Students are placed in the hospital and firm where they will be based for their FY1 training. During this time, they shadow the current FY1 doctor. Students complete their SSC programme and this may include spending time in a specialty not previously experienced or may allow them to gain a deeper understanding in an area that already interests them.

Throughout the year, students return to the medical school for a teaching programme; in addition, there are individual sessions in communication skills teaching and simulated patient scenarios. Students also complete their Intermediate Life Support qualification.

On successful completion of final examinations, students complete a four-week elective and this is followed by a further four-week hospital placement shadowing the FY1 doctor they will be replacing following graduation.

Information from Barts and The London School of Medicine and Dentistry at Queen Mary, University of London, www.smd.qmul.ac.uk.

Integrated courses

Integrated courses are those where basic medical sciences are taught concurrently with clinical studies. Thus, this style is a compromise between a traditional course and a PBL course. Although these courses have patient contact from the start, there is huge variation in the amount of contact from school to school. In year 1, contact is quite often limited to local community visits, with the amount of patient contact increasing as the years progress. In any case, most students are quite happy with having only limited contact with patients in the first year, as they feel that at this point they do not have a sufficient clinical knowledge base to approach patients on the wards.

Course structure: University of Manchester (integrated)

Approach to learning and facilities

Manchester Medical School has extensive teaching facilities including lecture rooms, laboratories and equipment. Small group teaching is conducted in custom-built rooms and the dissection room allows for the study of whole body dissection, prosections, anatomical models, histology and images. Each teaching hospital has a clinical skills laboratory, allowing students to develop many clinical skills in the relative 'safety' of simulation. Communication skills are taught and tested with the help of 'simulated patients' (volunteers who can mimic various clinical situations and give feedback to students). Clinical and communication skills are then systematically tested in examinations.

A central feature of the curriculum at Manchester is the use of mixed teaching and learning methods including lectures, problem-based and laboratory practical classes, dissection and, importantly, clinical learning right from the start of the course.

PBL is a key element of the programme. In PBL a group of students leads the learning with guidance from a tutor. The learning is focused on a clinically based scenario and in this way it sets the student up for a medical career in which a great deal of learning comes from interacting with a patient and the problems with which they present to the doctor. Because this approach is so different from learning at school or college, a study skills induction is run at the beginning of year 1 to prepare students for the transition into learning at university.

Students are guided to apply their biological, behavioural and social science learning to real patients from the start of the course and to move rapidly towards gaining wide clinical experience, using real clinical situations as a stimulus to learn. Students are encouraged to think of the whole teaching hospital and its surrounding community as a huge and readily available resource for their learning, with no boundaries or barriers. The hospitals operate 'sign-up schemes' to match up manageable numbers of interested students with appropriate specialist learning opportunities. Students receive comprehensive clinical teaching (with a strong emphasis on clinical skills/competence), building in intensity from year 1 through to year 5.

MBChB five-year programme

The five-year MBChB programme comprises three phases. Together these phases form the Manchester curriculum and each is informed by the three key themes of doctor as scholar and scientist, doctor as practitioner and doctor as professional. The modules in phase 1 of the programme lead on to the modules in phase 2, so there is a continuous progression from learning in the basic sciences to clinical sciences later on.

Phase 1

Year 1 begins with a module on 'life cycle' in semester 1 and continues with 'cardiorespiratory fitness' in semester 2. Year 2 starts with a module on 'mind and movement' in semester 3 and finishes with a module on 'nutrition and metabolism' in semester 4. Throughout years 1 and 2, students have early experience of clinical and community placements, which provides them with an introduction to health and illness and a professional context for their studies. In addition to this, there is the Personal Excellence Path (PEP), which allows students to focus on specific topics in more depth, while equipping them with the necessary research and analytical skills required in medicine.

Phase 2

Phase 2 is delivered in four health education zones (HEZ). Each HEZ is focused on one of the big teaching hospitals in the university cities of Manchester, Salford and Preston and incorporates teaching in district general hospitals and also in general practice. Students are randomly assigned to an HEZ shortly after the start of the first semester in phase 1.

Year 3 starts with an 'introduction to clinical learning' course during which there is a strong emphasis on the skills needed every time a student meets a patient. The remainder of year 3 consists of two modules: 'heart, lungs and blood' and 'nutrition, metabolism and excretion'. The majority of the year is spent on these core modules, but students will also continue to expand their knowledge on the PEP, focusing on the importance of quality improvement in modern healthcare.

Year 4 has two modules: 'mind and movement' and 'families and children'. In addition, there is one PEP module, where the research skills learned over the previous years are applied to an end of year project. This requires every student to carry out an extended study into a specific area. During both years students will spend a significant amount of time on community placements.

Phase 3

Year 5 of the programme includes a traditional elective period (StEP), at least one community module and two or more hospital modules (teaching hospital and district general hospital). An exemption exam takes place in January. Students who pass this exam will not have to sit the final exam at the end of the year. Following exams, students will undertake at least one student assistantship. Year 5 is the time to bring together what students have learned and put the finishing touches to clinical competence, in preparation for the foundation years. There is a strong emphasis on clinical apprenticeship, while giving students meaningful choices over their clinical attachments. It is also expected of them to shadow the doctor whose job they will take when they enter the Foundation programme.

There is the opportunity to work abroad in a partner European hospital in year 5.

MBChB six-year programme

This programme follows the same outline as the MBChB five-year programme but includes a foundation year for students who do not have the required science qualifications for entry into year 1. The foundation year provides an introduction into enquiry-based learning as well as extending the scientific knowledge and skills required for entry into year 1. Although the majority of the programme will be delivered at the medical school, much of the didactic teaching will be undertaken at Xaverian College, Manchester. Entry to year 1 of the five-year programme is automatic on satisfactory completion of the foundation year.

Reprinted with kind permission from the University of Manchester, www. manchester.ac.uk.

Intercalated degrees

Students who perform well in the examinations at the end of their preclinical studies (year 2 or 3) often take up the opportunity to complete an intercalated degree. An intercalated degree gives you the opportunity to incorporate a further degree (BSc or BA) into your medical course. This is normally a one-year project, during which students have the opportunity to investigate a chosen topic in much more depth, producing a final written thesis before rejoining the main course. Usually, a range of degrees are available to choose from, such as those from the traditional sciences, i.e. biochemistry, anatomy, physiology, or in topics as different as medical law, ethics, journalism and/or history of medicine.

Further features of an intercalated degree include the following.

- Anatomy continues to be taught using whole body dissection.
- Students will complete two degrees over the five years: the Bachelor of Medical Sciences in year 3 and the medical degrees (Bachelor of Medicine, Bachelor of Surgery) in year 5.
- The research component of the BMedSci degree provides students with excellent experience in research, with the opportunity of publishing papers.
- A professional approach is taken to training in that it uses procedures that are employed in the assessment of doctors after they graduate.
- The clinical training component of the course sees the amalgamation of students from the year 4 and 5 courses, which enhances the educational experience for both groups.

Why intercalate?

- It gives you the chance to study a particular subject in depth.
- It gives you the chance to be involved in research or lab work, particularly if you are interested in research later on.
- It gives you an advantage over other candidates if you later decide to specialise; for example, intercalating in anatomy would be useful if you wish to pursue a career in surgery.

Why not intercalate?

- The main drawback is the extra cost and time involved in taking a detour in your studies. This needs to be considered carefully.
- You could forget some of the things you've learned in the previous years of your medical degree, and thus will need to spend time reacquainting yourself with the forgotten material.

TIP!

Websites with further information about intercalated degrees:

- www.intercalate.co.uk
- www.smd.qmul.ac.uk/undergraduate/intercalated (Barts and The London School of Medicine and Dentistry).

Taking an elective

Towards the end of the course there is often the opportunity to take an elective study period, usually for two months, when students are expected to undertake a short project but are free to travel to any hospital or clinic in the world that is approved by their university. This gives you the opportunity to practise medicine anywhere in the world during your clinical years. For example, electives range from running clinics in developing countries to accompanying flying doctors in Australia. Students see this as an opportunity to do some travelling and visit exotic locations far from home before they qualify. You can also, if you want, opt to do an elective at home. If you want to know more about this, go to www.worktheworld.co.uk.

Postgraduate courses

There is a huge variety of opportunities and courses for further postgraduate education and training in medicine. This reflects the array of possible areas for specialisation. Medical schools and hospitals run a wide range of postgraduate programmes, which include further clinical and non-clinical training and research degree programmes.

Advice and guidance are available from the Royal College of Physicians (RCP) (www.rcplondon.ac.uk/medical-careers-training/postgraduate-exams) and the individual universities. As before, you will need to check the prospectuses of individual universities for the most up-to-date information.

Examples of postgraduate courses

The following postgraduate courses are offered by the University of Nottingham:

- Advanced Clinical Practice (MSc)
- Advanced Dietetic Practice (MSc)
- Anaesthesia and Intensive Care (DM/PHD)
- Clinical Microbiology (MSc)
- Practice Teacher in Health and Social Care (PGCert)
- Rehabilitation Psychology (MSc)
- Research Methods (Health) (MA)
- Research Methods (Science, Technology and Society) (MA)
- Sports and Exercise Medicine (MSc).

Source: www.nottingham.ac.uk
Reprinted with kind permission of the University of Nottingham

---

As you will see from the example course descriptions, all medical school courses cover the same essential information but can vary widely in their teaching styles; this is an important point to consider when choosing which course to apply to. Chapter 2 has further guidance on what to consider when choosing your university and course.

2 | Applying to study medicine

Getting an interview is essential because most medical schools only issue conditional offers after their admissions panel has met you. The evidence that the selector uses when he or she makes the choice to call you for interview or reject you is your UCAS application, which means that your application is the first vital step in getting into medical school. This chapter will guide you through the different parts of your application, including choosing where to apply, admissions tests and academic ability.

Some sections of the application are purely factual (your name, address, exam results, etc.). There is also a section where you enter your choice of medical schools. The personal statement section gives you an opportunity to write about yourself, and there is a space for your teacher to write a reference describing your strengths and weaknesses. Later in this book, you will find advice on how to fill in these sections and how to influence your referee, but first let's consider what happens, or might happen, to your application.

What happens to your application

Typically, a medical school might receive between 1,500 and 2,000 applications, almost all of which will arrive in September and October. The applications are distributed to the selectors, who have to decide which applicants to recommend for interview. The selectors will usually be busy doctors, and the task of selecting promising candidates means a good deal of extra work for them, on top of the usual demands of their full-time jobs. Most of the candidates will have been predicted grades that will allow them to be considered but the medical school can interview perhaps only 15% to 25% of them.

A high proportion of applicants will have good GCSE and AS results and predicted grades at A level of AAA or higher. (NB: nearly all universities now ask for three A grades and some for an A* grade.) They will also have undertaken some voluntary work or work-shadowing. In order to decide who should be called for interview, the selectors will have to make a decision based solely on the information provided by you and your school. If you are not called for interview, you will not be offered a place at that medical school. If your application does not convince the selector that you are the right sort of person to be a doctor, he or she will reject you. However outstanding your personal qualities are, unless your application is convincing, you will not be called for interview. This part of the guide is designed to maximise your chances of getting the interview even under the worst circumstances.

Deciding where to apply

There are 32 medical schools or university departments of medicine in the UK. They offer a range of options for students wishing to study medicine:

- five- or six-year MBBS or MBChB courses (UCAS codes A100 or A106)
- four-year accelerated graduate-entry courses (A101 or A102)
- six-year courses that include a 'pre-med' year (A103 or A104).

Entry requirements of all medical schools are summarised in Table 10 (see pages 152–154).

You can apply to up to four medical schools in one application cycle. In deciding which ones to eliminate, you may find the following points helpful.

- **Grades and retakes.** If you are worried that you will not achieve AAA grades the first time round, include at least three schools that accept retake candidates (see Table 10 on pages 152–154). The reason for this is that if you make a good impression at interview this year, you may not need to face a second interview at your next attempt. You will also be able to show loyalty by applying twice to the same school. Many medical schools will only consider second-time applicants if they applied to them originally.
- **Interviews.** A few medical schools do not interview A level candidates. If you think that you will be a much stronger candidate on your application form than in person, it may be advantageous to include these schools. Each school's interview rates are shown in Table 11 (see page 155).
- **Location and socialising.** You may be attracted to the idea of being at a campus university rather than at one of the medical schools that are not located on the campuses of their affiliated universities. One reason for this may be that you would like to mix with students from a wide variety of disciplines and that you will enjoy the intellectual and social cross-fertilisation. The trouble with this theory is that medical students work longer hours than most other students and tend to form a clique. Be warned: in reality you could find that you have little time to mix with non-medics.

- **Course structure.** While all the medical schools are well equipped and provide a high standard of teaching, there are real differences in the way the courses are taught and examined. Specifically, the majority offer an integrated course in which students see patients at an early stage and certainly before the formal clinical part of the course. The other main distinction is between systems-based courses, which teach medicine in terms of the body's systems (e.g. the cardiovascular system), and subject-based courses, which teach in terms of the fundamental subjects (anatomy, biochemistry, etc.) (see page 8).
- **Teaching style.** The style of teaching can also vary from place to place. See pages 7–14 for more information on PBL, integrated and traditional approaches to teaching.
- **Intercalated degrees and electives.** Another difference in the courses offered concerns the opportunities for an intercalated Honours BSc and electives. The intercalated BSc scheme allows students to tack on one further year of study either to the end of the two-year pre-clinical course or as an integrated part of a six-year course. Successful completion of this year, which may be used to study a wide variety of subjects, confers a BSc degree qualification. Electives are periods of work experience away from the medical school and, in some cases, abroad. See pages 14–16 for more information.

When choosing where to apply you should consult the medical schools' websites and prospectuses. Once you have narrowed the choice down to about 10 or 12, it is worth writing to all those on your list for a copy of their prospectus (these will be sent to you free of charge) and taking a good look at their websites.

The fifth choice

Although you can apply to a total of five institutions through UCAS, you may apply to only four medical schools; if you enter more than four, your application will be rejected. The question is: what should you do with the other slot? The medical schools will assure you that you can apply for other, non-medical courses without jeopardising your application to medicine, but I would advise you to think carefully before doing so, for the reasons given below.

- There's no point in thinking about alternatives if you really want to become a doctor.
- If you are unlucky and receive no conditional offers for medicine, you may have to accept an offer from your 'insurance' course.
- You might find it harder to convince your interviewers that you are completely committed to a career in medicine if you appear to be

happy to accept a place to study, say, chemical engineering or archaeology. The selectors cannot see what your other choices are but you will find it difficult to write a personal statement that appeals to both medical admissions tutors and those for another subject and you risk being rejected by all of your choices if you try to cover all subjects in your personal statement.

Having said this, there have been many students who apply for biomed courses as their fifth choice. If they are unsuccessful in their initial application this has often proved a way into medical school in future years.

The one reason to put a non-medical choice on your form is if you are not prepared to wait a year if your application is unsuccessful, and you intend to enter medicine as a graduate (see page 110).

Applying to Oxbridge medical schools

Oxbridge is in a separate category because, if getting into most medical schools is difficult, entry into Oxford or Cambridge is even more so (the extra hurdles facing students wishing to apply to Oxford or Cambridge are discussed in *Getting into Oxford & Cambridge*, another guide in this series). The general advice given here also applies to Oxbridge, but the competition is intense, and before you include either university on your UCAS application you need to be confident that you can achieve three A grades at A level and that you will interview well.

> **TIP!**
>
> You should discuss an application to Oxford or Cambridge with your teachers at an early stage.

You cannot apply to both Oxford and Cambridge in your application and your teachers will advise you whether to apply to either. You would need a good reason to apply to Oxbridge against the advice of your teachers and it certainly is not worth applying on the 'off chance' of getting in. By doing so you will simply waste one of your valuable four choices.

> **What the selector looks for**
>
> Most medical schools use a form that the selector fills in as he or she reads through your application. Have a look at the example form given in Figure 1; the next part of the chapter will examine each heading on this form in more detail.

MEDICAL INTERVIEW SELECTION FORM

Name: UCAS number:
Age at entry: Gap year?:
Selector: Date:

SELECTION CRITERIA COMMENTS

1   Academic (score out of 10)
GCSE results/AS grades/A level predictions
UKCAT/BMAT result

2   Commitment (score out of 10)
Genuine interest in medicine?
Relevant work experience?
Community involvement?

3   Personal (score out of 10)
Range of interests?
Involvement in school activities?
Achievements and/or leadership?
Referee supports application?

Total score (maximum of 30):

Recommendation of selector:	Interview	Score 25–30
	Reserve list	Score 16–24
	Rejection	Score 0–15

Further comments (if any):

Figure 1: Sample candidate selection form

Academic ability

GCSE results: points total and breadth of subjects

By the time you read this you will probably have chosen your GCSE subjects or even taken them. If you have not, here are some points to bear in mind.

Medical school selectors like to see breadth. Try to take as many GCSE subjects as possible. Try to take at least eight, but if your school places restrictions on the choice or number of GCSEs you take, make this clear in your personal statement.

- You will almost certainly need to study two science/maths subjects at A level, and you will need to study chemistry. There is a big gap between GCSE and A level. If you have the choice, don't make that jump even harder by studying combined or integrated science rather than the single science subjects. If your school will not allow you to study the single subjects, you should consider taking extra lessons during the summer holiday after your GCSE exams.
- Medical school selectors look at applicants' GCSE grades in con-siderable detail. Many medical schools ask for a 'good' set of GCSE results. What does this mean? Well, it varies from university to university, but a minimum of five A/B grades plus good grades in English language and mathematics are likely to be required. Some medical schools ask for a minimum of six A or A* grades at GCSE. Some specify the grades that they require, while others use the points system.
- If you have already taken your GCSEs and achieved disappointing grades, you must resign yourself to working exceptionally hard from the first day of your A level course. You will also need to convince your referee that the GCSE grades are not an indicator of low grades at A level, so that this can be mentioned in your reference.

AS levels: do they matter?

Under the current AS and A level system, there is a lot of pressure on you from the start of your two-year courses, since not only do the AS level grades appear on your application, but also many of the medical schools will specify minimum grade requirements. Even those that don't will consciously or subconsciously use them as an indicator of your likely A level grades. Imagine the situation: the selector has one more interview slot to fill, and has the choice between two students with iden-tical work experience, GCSE results and A level predictions, but one scored BBBB at AS level and the other achieved AAAA. Who do you think will get the place? The other thing to bear in mind is that a low score at AS level – C grades, say – is unlikely to lead to AAA at A level since an AS contributes up to 50% of the total A level marks, and so the selectors may doubt that the predicted grades (see below) are achievable.

You must be aware of the importance of retaking AS units if possible. Every extra mark gained on the (easier) AS units is a mark that you don't have to get in the (harder) A2 exams. If you have a second attempt at an AS unit, the board will take the higher of the two marks.

A level predictions

Your choice of A levels

You will see from Table 10 (pages 152–154) that most medical schools now ask for just two science/maths subjects at A level, with another science at AS level. They all require chemistry and/or biology so you need to choose either physics or mathematics if you wish to apply to a medical school that requires three science/maths subjects. There are three important considerations.

1. Choose subjects that you are good at. You must be capable of an A grade. If you aren't sure, ask your teachers.
2. Choose subjects that will help you in your medical course; life at medical school is tough enough as it is without having to learn new subjects from scratch.
3. While it is acceptable to choose a non-scientific third AS or A level that you enjoy and that will provide you with an interesting topic of conversation at your interview, you should be careful not to choose subjects such as art, which is practical rather than academic. General studies is not acceptable either. However, students who can cope with the differing demands of arts and sciences at A level have an advantage in that they can demonstrate breadth.

So what combination of subjects should you choose? In addition to chemistry/biology and another science at A level, you might also consider subjects such as psychology, sociology or a language at AS level. The point to bear in mind when you are making your choices is that you need high grades, so do not pick a subject that sounds interesting, such as Italian, if you are not good at languages. Similarly, although an AS level in statistics might look good on your UCAS application, you will not do well at it if you struggled at GCSE mathematics. You will need to check the individual requirements, but in general it is likely that most medical schools will prefer at least one AS level to be in an arts or humanities subject.

Taking four A levels

There's no harm in doing more than three A levels or four AS levels, but you should drop the fourth/fifth subject if there is any danger of it pulling down your grades in the others. Medical schools will not include the fourth A level in any conditional offers they make.

If you are taking the International Baccalaureate, then you should still be aiming to take biology and chemistry as these are the subjects required for undergraduate study. However, some universities specify chemistry and one of mathematics, biology, human biology and physics. If you are not taking these subjects you should be considering what makes you think you will be able to cope on a medicine course. For Scottish students, you are expected to have at least two Advanced Highers and three Highers, with biology and chemistry to at least Higher level; Imperial College, for example, asks for five Highers and three Advanced Highers to A grade standard. Overall, students should be aiming for majority A grades in Highers and Advanced Highers, though AB at Advanced Highers is accepted.

The prediction

The selector will look for a grade prediction in the reference that your teacher writes about you. Your teacher will probably make a prediction based on the reports of your subject teachers, your GCSE grades and, most importantly, on the results of the school exams and AS levels that you take at the end of year 12.

Consequently, it is vital that you work hard during the first year of A levels. Only by doing so will you get the reference you need. If there is any reason or excuse to explain why you did badly at GCSE or did not work hard in year 12, you must make sure that the teacher writing your reference knows about it and includes it in the reference. The most common reasons for poor performance are illness and problems at home (e.g. illness of a close relation or family breakdown).

The bottom line is that you need to persuade your school that you are on track for grades of AAA. Convincing everyone else usually involves convincing yourself!

Aptitude tests

Some universities ask applicants to sit aptitude tests as part of the application process. These tests include the UKCAT and BMAT tests.

UKCAT (the UK Clinical Aptitude Test)

The UKCAT has been adopted by 27 universities as part of their admissions procedures, and helps them make an informed choice between the highest candidates for undergraduate medical study. It is designed to ensure that students have the mental capabilities, attitude and professional conduct required for a career in the medical field. It is not a test of your curriculum knowledge or any scientific background. The UKCAT tests thought processes and as such cannot be revised for. It is a computer-based test but needs to be sat at an official centre. Test centres can be found in many locations worldwide. If there is a problem with you attending any of these centres, you should consult the UKCAT website (www.ukcat.ac.uk).

There are four sections to the UKCAT. These sections are based on a set of skills that medical (and dental) schools believe are vital to be successful as a medical practitioner. The four sections are listed below.

1. **Verbal reasoning.** Candidates are provided with a piece of text that they have to analyse and answer questions on.
2. **Quantitative reasoning.** The candidate's ability to deal with numerical questions is tested.
3. **Abstract reasoning.** Candidates have to draw relationships from written information.
4. **Decision analysis.** Information is given to the candidate in various forms. The candidate must use this to make informed assessments of the material and then make an appropriate response.

From 2011 onwards the test stopped testing behavioural trait analysis, which was section 5. In 2012 UKCAT ran a pilot scheme to add another assessment of Situational Judgement, testing candidates' judgement of medical-related situations. You will need to check to confirm if this has been formally added to the UKCAT test.

The test lasts 1 hour and 30 minutes.

The questions from all four sections are multiple choice and are divided up as follows.

- Verbal reasoning comprises 44 questions and lasts 22 minutes.
- Quantitative reasoning has 36 questions and lasts 23 minutes.
- Abstract reasoning has 65 questions in 16 minutes.
- Decision analysis comprises 26 questions in 26 minutes.

Those candidates with special educational needs are given longer (about 25% more time) for each set of questions.

Dates

A list of important dates regarding the UKCAT exam can be found on their website at www.ukcat.ac.uk. For those students wishing to apply for entry in 2014, the most important ones are as follows:

- registration deadline: 20 September 2013
- last testing date: 4 October 2013.

Universities that require the UKCAT

Table 5 shows the UK universities that require students to sit the UKCAT as part of their application process.

Table 5 Medical schools requiring UKCAT admissions test

Medical school	UCAS course code
University of Aberdeen	A100, A201
Brighton and Sussex Medical School	A100
Barts and The London School of Medicine and Dentistry	A100, A101, A200, A201
Cardiff University	A100, A101, A104, A200, A204
University of Dundee	A100, A104, A200, A204
University of Durham	A100
University of East Anglia	A100, A104
University of Edinburgh	A100
University of Glasgow	A100, A200
Hull York Medical School	A100
Keele University	A100, A104
King's College London	A100, A101, A102, A202, A205, A206
Imperial College London Graduate Entry	A101
University of Leeds	A100
University of Leicester	A100, A101
University of Manchester	A104, A106, A204, A206
University of Newcastle	A100, A101, A206
University of Nottingham	A100, A108
University of Oxford Graduate Entry	A101
Peninsula College of Medicine and Dentistry	A100
Queen's University Belfast	A100, A200
Queen Mary University	A100, A101, A200, A201
University of Sheffield	A100, A104, A200
University of Southampton	A100, A101, A102
University of St Andrews	A100, A990, B900
St George's, University of London	A100, A900
Warwick University Graduate Entry	A101

Preparation

Although the UKCAT website tries to discourage students from doing any preparation for the test other than sitting the practice test available online, students who have sat the test in the past have found that the more practice they had on timed IQ-type tests, the better prepared they felt. In the reference section of most bookshops there are a number of books that contain practice questions of a similar type to the UKCAT.

General hints

- Use the practice tests provided to familiarise yourself with the type of questions that are asked and the time constraints in the test.
- Most candidates do not complete all sections in the test so don't worry if you don't. Use the practice test to ensure that you know how to pace yourself. Try to answer all of the questions but don't worry if you don't get to the end of each section.
- There is a point for each right answer, but no points are deducted for wrong answers.
- Try not to leave blanks. If you really can't work out the answer, it is better to eliminate the answers that you know to be wrong and then make your best guess from those that are left.
- Leave enough time to guess the remaining questions. My advice would be one minute.
- Be aware that if you have not viewed the whole screen of the question that you are on, you cannot move onto the next question or go back to any of the questions you have answered. There are both vertical and horizontal scroll bars.
- Finally, it is most important that you stay calm in the test. Prepare yourself, pace yourself and move on if you're struggling with particular questions. It is inevitable that you will find some questions and some sections easier than others.

Sample UKCAT questions

All sample UKCAT questions reprinted with kind permission of UKCAT and Pearson Vue.

Verbal reasoning

In this section you will be presented with some text (an example is shown below) and given four statements relating to each passage.

Sample UKCAT verbal reasoning question

In digital recording, the analogue sound that we hear needs to be translated into a series of numbers ('0' or '1'). These numbers represent the changes in air pressure over time that make up the sound, though we cannot directly hear these numbers as sound.

Digital recordings are made by sending the original analogue sound to an 'analogue to digital converter' (ADC). This converter changes the analogue signal to a series of binary numbers. These numbers are then usually stored in a computer or on a compact disc. During

---

playback, the digital sound information is read and sent to a 'digital to analogue converter' (DAC), which changes the sound into an analogue signal that is reproduced by devices such as a loudspeaker or headphones.

For each statement, you must choose an answer from 'true', 'false' and 'can't tell' based on the information you are given in the passage.

A loudspeaker is able to produce an analogue signal.

A. True

B. False

C. Can't tell

Quantitative reasoning

For the quantitative reasoning section you are presented with numerical data (see the example below).

Sample UKCAT numerical data table

A distribution centre serves stores within a 50-mile radius. The table below shows how far each store is from the distribution centre.

Distance from distribution centre	Number of stores
10 miles or less	3
11 to 20 miles	15
21 to 30 miles	26
31 to 40 miles	20
41 to 50 miles	16

You will be given four statements where you must choose one correct answer.

How many stores does the distribution centre serve?

A. 60

B. 70

C. 80

D. 90

E. Can't tell

Abstract reasoning

This is a slightly shorter section and, according to the UKCAT website, it 'assesses candidates' ability to infer relationships from information by convergent and divergent thinking'.

For each question you will be presented with two sets of shapes, A and B (see Figures 2 and 3).

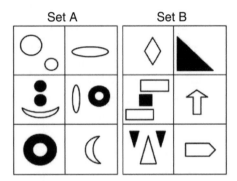

Figure 2 Sample UKCAT abstract reasoning shape sets

For each set, you will be presented with five test shapes, for example:

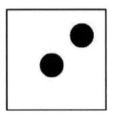

A. Set A   B. Set B   C. Neither

Figure 3 Sample UKCAT abstract reasoning answer choices

You have to decide if this belongs to set A or set B.

Decision analysis

This section, according to the UKCAT website, is designed to 'assess [your] ability to deal with various forms of information, to infer relationships, to make informed judgements and to decide on an appropriate response in situations of complexity and ambiguity'.

Sample UKCAT decision analysis code table

Additional codes

Operators general rules	Specific info basic codes	Complex info additional information	Reactions/ outcomes/ emotions
A = positive	1 = personal	101 = speed	201 = hurt
B = increase	2 = people	102 = injury	202 = excited
C = opposite	3 = air	103 = danger	203 = worried
D = cold	4 = fire	104 = fun	204 = angry
E = fast	5 = water	105 = carry	205 = surprise
F = generalise	6 = earth	106 = empty	
G = combine	7 = sun		
	8 = moon		
	9 = dwelling		
	10 = move		
	11 = today		
	12 = light		
	13 = bag		
	14 = look		

You will then have 26 questions to answer based on the information in this table. Each question will have four or five possible answers; see the example below.

What is the best interpretation of the following coded message?

11, 12, 7

A. Today it is bright and sunny

B. The light from the sun is brighter than usual

C. Today the sun came up

D. Today the sun's rays have a strange hue

E. The sun is floating in the sky

Answers to all questions are on page 48

BMAT (BioMedical Admissions Test)

The BMAT is a test to ensure effective selection of well-qualified students. At present, five medical schools use this test (as outlined in Table 6): Cambridge, Imperial, Lee Kong Chian School of Medicine (part of Imperial College), Oxford and University College London (UCL).

Table 6 Medical schools requiring BMAT admissions test

Medical school	UCAS course code
University of Cambridge	A100, A101
Imperial College London	A100, B900, B9N2
Lee Kong Chian	MBBS
University of Oxford	A100, A101, BC98
University College London	A100

This is a written test and is deemed a productive indicator of a student's likely result in their first year of undergraduate study.

All candidates applying to these institutions or courses are required to take the BMAT.

The test, which takes place in November, consists of three sections.

1. aptitude and skills (60 minutes – 35 multiple-choice or short-answer questions)
2. scientific knowledge and applications (30 minutes – 27 multiple-choice or short-answer questions)
3. writing task (30 minutes – one from a choice of three short essay questions).

Sample BMAT question

BMAT specimen paper

Section 1: Aptitude and skills question 3

Doctors in Great Britain can work for the public health service, a commercial service, or both. 30% of doctors in Great Britain work, at least some of the time, for the commercial sector. On the basis of this information alone, deduce which of the following statements are true of doctors in Great Britain.

1. Some doctors work only in the public health service.
2. More doctors work in the public health service than the commercial sector.
3. Some doctors spend more time on commercial work than in the public health service.

A. 1 only
B. 2 only
C. 1 and 2 only
D. 2 and 3 only
E. 1, 2 and 3

Answer on page 48

From the specimen papers available on the Admissions Testing Service website (www.admissionstestingservice.org). Reprinted by permission of the University of Cambridge Local Examinations Syndicate.

General hints

- Familiarity with the basic structure of the test is good preparation – however, it is not a test you can revise for.
- Do not waste your money paying for a tutor to help you learn for this, it is testing your ability.
- As with the UKCAT, the majority of candidates do not complete all sections in the test so don't worry if you don't. Ensure that you have tried the practice tests first so that you understand the timing of the test. Try to answer as many questions as you can but do not worry if you do not get to the end of each section.
- In sections 1 and 2, there is a point for each right answer, but no points are deducted for wrong answers.
- In section 3, each of the essays are double marked and there is a mark for the quality of written English presentation.
- Try your best to avoid leaving unanswered questions. Read the question thoroughly to try and work out what the possible answer could be by ruling out other answers.
- It might be obvious but the best thing you can do is stay calm. If you have put in the time to practise beforehand then you have prepared as best you can. Do not ruin your chances by letting nerves get in your way.

Commitment

Have you shown a genuine interest in medicine?

This question has to be answered partly by your reference and partly by you in your personal statement but, before we go on, it's time for a bit of soul-searching in the form of a short test, found below. Get a piece of paper and do this immediately, before you read on.

The Getting into Medical School genuine interest test

Answer all the questions truthfully.

- Do you regularly read the following for articles about medicine?

  o   daily broadsheet newspapers

  o   *New Scientist*

  o   *Student BMJ*

  o   www.bbc.co.uk/health.

- Do you regularly watch medical dramas and current affairs programmes such as *Panorama* or *Newsnight*?

- Do you possess any books or CD-ROMs about the human body or medicine, or do you visit medical websites?
- Have you attended a first-aid course?
- Have you arranged a visit to your local GP?
- Have you arranged to visit your local hospital in order to see the work of doctors at first hand?
- What day of the week does your favourite newspaper publish a health section?
- Do you know the main causes of death in this country?
- Do you know what the following stand for?

  o   GMC
  o   BMA
  o   NICE
  o   AIDS
  o   SARS
  o   MMR
  o   MRSA
  o   H5N1.

You should have answered 'yes' to most of the first six questions and should have been able to give answers to the last three. A low score (mainly 'no' and 'don't know' answers) should make you ask yourself whether you really are sufficiently interested in medicine as a career. If you achieved a high score, you need to ensure that you communicate your interest in your UCAS application. The chapter will soon go on to explain how, but first a note about work experience and courses.

Have you done relevant work experience and courses?

It is always advisable to arrange your own work experience, and it is perfectly reasonable to use contacts, whether family members or friends, but medical schools will not want to see in your personal statement that you have shadowed a parent after they arranged the work experience for you. Organisational abilities are a vital component of becoming a doctor. This could be used as an important method of proving that you have the necessary skill set.

In addition to making brief visits to your local hospital and GP's surgery (which you should be able to arrange through your school or with the help of your parents), it is important to undertake a longer period of relevant work experience. If possible, try to get work experience that involves the gritty, unglamorous side of patient care. A week spent helping elderly and confused patients walk to the toilet is worth a month in the hospital laboratory helping the technicians carry out routine tests. Unfortunately, these hospital jobs are hard to get, and you may have to offer to work at weekends or at night. If that fails, you should try your local hospice or care home.

Hospices tend to be short of money because they are maintained by voluntary donations. They are usually happy to take on conscientious volunteers, and the work they do (caring for the terminally ill) is particularly appropriate. Remember that you are not only working in a hospital/ hospice in order to learn about medicine in action. You are also there to prove (to yourself as well as to the admissions tutors) that you have the dedication and stomach for what is often an unpleasant and upsetting work environment. You should be able to get the address of your nearest hospice from your GP's surgery or online.

> **TIP!**
>
> Because of health and safety regulations, it is not always possible to arrange work experience or voluntary work with GPs, in hospitals or in hospices. The medical schools' selectors are aware of this but they will expect you to have found alternatives.

Volunteer work with a local charity is a good way of demonstrating your commitment as well as giving you the opportunity to find out more about medicine. HIV/AIDS charities, for example, welcome volunteers. A spokesman for Positive East, the leading HIV/AIDS charity in east London, says:

> 'Volunteers play an essential role in delivering services, providing project support and raising essential funds and are central to the charity's operation. Volunteer roles are tailored to match individual needs and full training and support is provided. Research and work placements are also available.'

Contact details for Positive East can be found at the end of this book.

Any medical contact is better than none, so clerical work in a medical environment, work in a hospital magazine stall or voluntary work for a charity working in a medical-related area is better than no work experience at all. When you come to write the personal statement section of your UCAS application you will want to describe your practical experience of medicine in some detail. Say what you did, what you saw and what insights you gained from it. As always, include details that could provide the signpost to an interesting question in your interview.

For example, suppose you write: 'During the year that I worked on Sunday evenings at St Sebastian's Hospice, I saw a number of patients who were suffering from cancer and it was interesting to observe the treatment they received and watch its effects.' A generous interviewer will ask you about the management of cancer, and you have an opportunity to impress if you can explain the use of drugs, radiotherapy, diet, exercise and so on. The other benefit of work in a medical environment is that you may be able to make a good impression on the senior staff you have worked for. If they are prepared to write a brief reference and send it to your school, the teacher writing your reference will be able to quote from it.

Always keep a diary

During your work experience, keep a diary and write down what you see being done. At the time, you may think that you will remember what you saw, but it could be as long as 18 months between the work experience and an interview, and you will almost certainly forget vital details. Very often, applicants are asked at interview to expand on something interesting on their UCAS application. For example:

Interviewer: I see that you observed a coronary angioplasty. What does that involve?

Candidate: Er.

Interviewer: Well, I know it's hard to see what's happening but I'm sure you understand the reason for carrying out a coronary angioplasty.

Candidate: Um.

Don't allow this to happen to you!

A much better answer should go something like this . . .

Interviewer: I see that you observed a coronary angioplasty. What does that involve?

Candidate: I did, at XYZ Hospital. I shadowed Dr X for a day. It is a procedure carried out when the coronary arteries that supply oxygen to the cardiac muscle become narrowed and blocked. An angioplasty involves inserting a catheter into the artery. The catheter has a small balloon on the end that is inflated at the site of the blockage called an atherosclerotic plaque. The catheter also contains a stent which is left in the artery to keep it open. The artery wall stretches and the blood can flow around the blockage and get to the muscle.

Interviewer: How will this help the patient?

Candidate: A lack of blood means a lack of oxygen to the heart. This will cause the heart to respire anaerobically and lactic acid can build up causing pain in the heart called angina and referred pain along the left arm and side of the body. It can lead to a heart attack. An increase in blood flow through these arteries will help prevent this from happening.

Interviewer: What is the prognosis? [This is very important to have developed in any answer of the type of 'what would you do?']

Candidate: Dr X stated that the patient has to return to hospital once a month as the artery walls are elastic and may narrow again. They are also advised to reduce the intake of saturated fats in the diet as these are likely to encourage the blockage to increase in size. With monitoring and dietary restrictions the treatment is quite successful. He stated it will help about 90% of patients with angina.

The only problem with work experience is that it can be hard to persuade members of a busy medical team to spend time explaining in detail what they are doing and why. MPW (Mander Portman Woodward school group) and Medlink and Future Doctors (see page 141) run courses for sixth-formers to help them understand the common areas of medicine and to link this theoretical knowledge to practical procedures.

Have you been involved in your local community?

A career in medicine involves serving the community, and you need to demonstrate that you have something of the dedication needed to be a good doctor. You may have been able to do this through voluntary jobs in hospitals or hospices. If not, you need to think about devoting a regular period each week to one of the charitable organisations that cares for those in need.

The number of organisations needing this help has increased following the government's decision to close some of the long-stay mental institutions and place the burden of caring for patients on local authorities. Your local social services department (their address should be in the phone book) will be able to give you information on this and other opportunities for voluntary work. Again, it is helpful to obtain brief references from the people you work for so that these can be included in what your teacher writes about you.

Making sure medicine is right for you

It is important to do your research into why medicine is indeed the right career choice for you. If you have chosen medicine for the wrong reasons, it is likely to come out at interview. There are short courses run by

M&D Experience and practising doctors at local hospitals who give an insight into medicine as a career. They do not intend to promote or glamorise medicine, but rather expose it as a profession. This might be an excellent way to assess your motivation at an early stage and also act as part of your work experience in medicine, which would be a good talking point at interview to justify your career choice. See www.mdexperience.co.uk.

> 'When I read a personal statement, I am looking for a structured account of the journey the student has taken from his or her first idea about studying medicine, outlining the steps taken to investigate what a career in medicine involves. Structure and thorough research make much more of an impact than an "interesting" opening sentence. I am also looking for evidence that the student is a team player, that he or she takes an active role in extracurricular activities either in or out of school, and can demonstrate situations where communication with others is necessary. Closing statements, however well written, emphasising the student's commitment to medicine and his/her desire to contribute to the life of the medical school simply waste space that could be used to discuss work experience or voluntary work.'
>
> Admissions tutor

Personal qualities

Have you demonstrated a range of interests?

Medical schools like to see applicants who have done more with their life than work for their A levels and watch TV. While the teacher writing your reference will probably refer to your outstanding achievements in his or her reference, you also need to say something about your achievements in your personal statement. Selectors like to read about achievements in sport and other outdoor activities, such as the Duke of Edinburgh's Award Scheme. Equally useful activities include Young Enterprise, charity work, public speaking, part-time jobs, art, music and drama.

Bear in mind that selectors will be asking themselves: 'Would this person be an asset to the medical school?' Put in enough detail and try to make it interesting to read.

Here is an example of a good paragraph on interests for the personal statement section:

> 'I very much enjoy tennis and play in the school team and for Hampshire at under-18 level. This summer a local sports shop has sponsored me to attend a tennis camp in California. I worked at

the Wimbledon championships in 2007. I have been playing the piano since the age of eight and took my Grade 7 exam recently. At school, I play in the orchestra and in a very informal jazz band. Last year I started learning the trombone but I would not like anyone except my teacher to hear me playing! I like dancing and social events but my main form of relaxation is gardening. I have started a small business helping my neighbours to improve their gardens – which also brings in some extra money.'

And here's how not to do it:

'I play tennis in competitions and the piano and trombone. I like gardening.'

But what if you aren't musical, can't play tennis and find geraniums boring? It depends when you are reading this. Anyone with enough drive to become a doctor can probably rustle up an interest or two in six months. If you haven't even got that long, then it would be sensible to devote most of your personal statement to your interest in medicine.

Have you contributed to school activities?

This is largely covered by the section on interests, but it is worth noting that the selector is looking for someone who will contribute to the communal life of the medical school. If you have been involved in organising things in your school, do remember to include the details. Don't forget to say that you ran the school's fundraising barbecue or that you organised a sponsored jog in aid of disabled children – if you did so. Conversely, medical schools are less interested in applicants whose activities are exclusively solitary or cannot take place in the medical school environment. Don't expect to get much credit for:

'My main interest is going for long walks in desolate places by myself or in the company of my iPod.'

Have you any achievements or leadership experience to your credit?

You should bear in mind that the selectors are looking for applicants who stand out and who have done more with their lives than the absolute minimum. They are particularly attracted by excellence in any sphere. Have you competed in any activity at a high level or received a prize or other recognition for your achievements? Have you organised and led any events or team games? Were you elected as class representative to the school council? If so, make sure that you include it in your personal statement.

> **WARNING!**
> - Don't copy any of the paragraphs above onto your own UCAS application.
> - Don't write anything that isn't true.
> - Don't write anything you can't talk about at the interview.
> - Avoid over-complicated, over-formal styles of writing. Read your personal statement out loud; if it doesn't sound like you speaking, rewrite it.

The UCAS application

You will receive advice from your school on how to complete a UCAS application, and you may also find it helpful to consult *How to Complete Your UCAS Application*, another title in this series (see page 143 for details). Some additional points that apply chiefly to medicine are set out below.

When the medical school receives your UCAS application, it will not be on its own but in a batch, possibly of many. The selectors will have to consider it, along with the rest, in between the demands of other aspects of their jobs. If your application is badly worded, uninteresting or lacking the things that the selector feels are important, it will be put on the 'reject without interview' pile. A typical medical school might receive well over a thousand applications. Table 1 on page 2 shows the number of applicants in the 2011/12 application cycle for each of the medical schools. The number of applicants at each university has to then be reduced to those who will be interviewed.

You can only be called for interview on the basis of your UCAS application. The selectors will not know about the things that you have forgotten to say, and they can get an impression of you only from what is in the application. I have come across too many good students who never got an interview simply because they did not think properly about their personal statement; they relied on their hope that the selectors would somehow see through the words and get an instinctive feeling about them.

The following sections will tell you more about what the selectors are looking for, and how you can avoid common mistakes. Before looking at how the selectors go about deciding whom to call to interview, there are a number of important things that you need to think about.

The personal statement

The most important part of your application is your personal statement, as this is your chance to show the university selectors three very important themes. These are:

- why you want to be a doctor
- what you have done to investigate the profession
- whether you are the right sort of person for their medical school (in other words, the personal qualities that make you an outstanding candidate).

Thus the personal statement is your opportunity to demonstrate to the selectors that you not only have researched medicine thoroughly, but that you also have the right personal qualities to succeed as a doctor.

Do not be tempted to write the statement in the sort of formal English that you find in, for example, job applications. Read through a draft of your statement and ask yourself the question 'Does it sound like me?' If not, rewrite it. Avoid phrases such as 'I was fortunate enough to be able to shadow a doctor' when you really just mean 'I shadowed a doctor' or 'I arranged to shadow a doctor'.

Another important consideration is the fact that your personal statement needs to be no more than 47 lines long or 4,000 characters (including spaces); this is a strict limit and so you need to ensure that you are as close to this as possible.

The personal statement is your opportunity to demonstrate to the selectors that you are fully committed to studying medicine and have the right motivation and personal qualities to do so successfully. A typical personal statement takes time and effort to get right; don't expect perfection after one draft.

Why medicine?

Your personal statement must, fundamentally, convince admissions tutors of your interest in following a career in medicine.

A high proportion of UCAS applications contain a sentence like 'From an early age I have wanted to be a doctor because it is the only career that combines my love of science with the chance to work with people.' Not only do admissions tutors get bored with reading this, but it is also clearly untrue: if you think about it, there are many careers that combine science and people, including teaching, pharmacy, physiotherapy and nursing.

However, the basic ideas behind this sentence may well apply to you. If so, you need to personalise it. You could mention an incident that first got you interested in medicine – a visit to your own doctor, a conversation with a family friend, or a lecture at school, for instance. You could write about your interest in human biology or a biology project that you undertook when you were younger to illustrate your interest in science, and you could give examples of how you like to work with others. The important thing is to back up your initial interest with your efforts to investigate the career.

Presentation

The vast majority of applications are completed electronically through the UCAS website using the Apply system. The online system has many useful built-in safety checks to ensure that you do not make mistakes.

Despite the help that the electronic version provides, it is still possible to create an unfavourable impression on the selectors through spelling mistakes, grammatical errors and unclear personal statements. In order to ensure that this does not happen, follow these tips.

- Read the instructions for each section of the application carefully before filling it in.
- Double-check all dates (when you joined and left schools, when you sat examinations), examination boards, GCSE grades and personal details (fee codes, residential status codes, disability codes).
- Plan your personal statement as you would an essay. Lay it out in a logical order. Make the sentences short and to the point. Split the section into paragraphs, covering each of the necessary topics (i.e. work experience, reasons for choice, interests and achievements). This will enable the selector to read and assess it quickly and easily.
- Ask your parents, or someone who is roughly the same age as the selectors (over 30), to cast a critical eye over your draft, and don't be too proud to make changes in the light of their advice.

> **TIP!**
>
> Keep a copy of your personal statement so that you can look at it when you prepare for the interview.

A sample statement can be found below. It is a good personal statement made by a sixth form student. Don't be put off by someone else's experiences. You have your own style and achievements, and what you have to do is write the statement in a manner that captures the reader's imagination and leaves them under no illusion that you are primarily focused on medicine as a vocation for life. Here, the example demonstrates clarity and focus, and what comes through the most is the enthusiasm that the candidate has for medicine. These attributes will give the applicant an excellent chance of being called in for an interview and/or just being given an offer.

Personal statement

Character count (including spaces): 3,928

I am convinced that I want to study medicine. This has been re-inforced by three weeks of work experience in both primary and secondary care. I am confident that medicine and the application of science to help people is an area of life I would thrive in. I have seen medical practice first hand, know the application and hard work required to be a doctor, but believe that the privilege of being able to care for the sick, help solve problems and make a difference far outweighs these demands.

I organised two contrasting periods of work experience: the first was in vascular surgery at St Mary's Hospital, London. I was attached to a consultant, but spent most of my time with junior doctors, one of whom hated his job. This gave me some insight into the difficulties that trainees may face, and made me reflect on my career choice. I found GP work experience totally different to the hospital, but the contrasts between the roles was very interesting in terms of the doctor–patient relationships. I also worked at the Royal Infirmary and was exposed to all aspects of the hospital, from patient check-ups to histopathology, radiology and surgery, which helped me to make an informed decision as to my area of specialism in the future. Every other Sunday last year I helped a team of volunteers feeding the homeless. I found this rewarding, as it taught me the importance of social networks in community help. Dealing with difficult situations there has helped me to develop my empathy and communication skills. During my gap year I have become a trained phlebotomist, working at St Thomas' Hospital, London, and also work part time as a lifeguard, two jobs that I feel give me valuable experience ahead of pursuing my career in medicine.

My A level subjects have given me a sense of enthusiasm and passion about science. In physics I learnt a great deal preparing a presentation on human mechanics in sport. I find the largely medical and anatomical section of my biology course fascinating. I am also proud to have come top of my year in the GCSE astronomy course I did two years ago. As advertising officer for my school's medical society, I enjoyed writing for its magazine, giving talks and taking part in heated debates. This has helped me to complete my Gold Science Communicators award and further harnessed my interest and excitement to have a career in medicine. I am enthusiastic and well-organised, with the energy and motivation to pursue ambitious projects with success. At school I held several positions of responsibility. I was form captain in 2008/09 and as an elected senior committee member for the head girl team I managed the student prefects, developing ideas for competitions and organising the administration of them, alongside finding the time to follow a busy extracurricular sports and music schedule.

I took every opportunity to contribute to the wider school community. As captain of the school netball, swimming and waterpolo teams I have learnt leadership skills and how to appreciate and use my players' different qualities to build a successful team that trusts and values each other. I have recently been selected for a cheerleading squad outside school and have also played netball at a club for the last three years, regularly playing league matches. My contribution to sport was recognised when I was awarded the school's 'Senior Sportsperson of the Year' prize in 2009. I am an accomplished musician; I toured Germany with the London Youth Wind Band in 2008, won my school's 'Young Musician of the Year' competition in 2008 and in July 2010 I gained my Music Performance Diploma on clarinet. These activities have required dedication and commitment, qualities I know I will need as a doctor.

I am excited at the prospect of studying medicine. I know that this is a lifelong commitment, but I am prepared and eager for the hard work and challenges ahead. This is how I want to spend my future.

WARNING!

Do not write any of the above passages in your personal statement, as admissions tutors are all too aware of the existence of this book. They also use plagiarism software to determine similarities between scripts. Ensure that your personal statement is not only personal to you, but also honest.

The reference

The reference will be written by a referee who could be your headteacher, housemaster, personal tutor or director of studies. They will write about what an outstanding person you are and about your contribution to school life as well as your academic achievement (i.e. on target for at least three A grades at A level), and they will then also give reasons why you are suitable to study medicine. For them to say this it must of course be true, as referees have to be as honest as possible and they will accurately assess your character and potential to succeed at university. You must have demonstrated to your teachers and other members of staff that you have all the necessary qualities required to become a doctor. To start demonstrating this in your upper sixth year may well be too late – ideally these characteristics should have been evident over previous years.

To what extent does your referee support your application?

The vital importance of judicious grovelling to your referee and making sure that he or she knows all the good news about your work in hospitals and in the local community has already been explained. Remember that the teacher writing your reference will rely heavily on advice from other teachers too. They also need to be buttered up and helped to see you as a natural doctor. Come to school scrupulously clean and tidy. Work hard, look keen and make sure you talk about medicine in class. Ask intelligent, medicine-related questions such as those given below.

- Is it because enzymes become denatured at over 45°C that patients suffering from heatstroke have to be cooled down quickly using ice?
- Could sex-linked diseases such as muscular dystrophy be avoided by screening the sperm to eliminate those containing the X chromosomes that carry the harmful recessive genes from an affected male?

Your friends may find all this nauseating – ignore them.

If your referee is approachable, you should be able to ask whether or not he or she feels able to support your application. In the unlikely case that he or she cannot recommend you, you should consider asking if another teacher could complete the application; clashes of personality do very occasionally occur and you must not let the medical schools receive a reference that damns you.

As part of the reference your referee will need to predict the grades that you are likely to achieve. The entry requirements of the medical schools are shown in Table 10 on pages 152–154. If you are predicted lower than the requirements it is almost certain that you will not be considered.

If you are a mature student or going through graduate entry, the referee could be a lecturer from your university who will provide the appropriate information.

Timing

The UCAS submission period is from 1 September to 15 January, but medical applications have to be with UCAS by 15 October. Late applications are also permitted, although medical schools are not bound to consider them. It is recommended that students thoroughly check university websites to ensure that the given dates are correct. Remember that most referees take at least a week to consult the relevant teachers and compile a reference, so allow for that and aim to submit your application by 1 September unless there is a good reason for delaying.

The only convincing reason for delaying is that your teachers cannot predict high A level grades at the moment, but might be able to do so if they see high-quality work during the autumn term. If you are not on track for AAA by October, you still need to submit your application because, without an entry in the UCAS system, you cannot participate in Clearing.

What happens next and what to do about it

Once your reference has been submitted, a receipt will be sent to your school or college to acknowledge its arrival. Your application is then processed and UCAS will send you confirmation of your details. If you don't receive this, you should check with your referee that it has been correctly submitted. The confirmation will contain your application number, your details and the list of courses to which you have applied.

Check carefully to make sure that the details in your application have been saved to the UCAS system correctly. At the same time, make a note of your UCAS number – you will need to quote this when you contact the medical schools.

Now comes a period of waiting, which can be very unsettling but which must not distract you from your studies. Most medical schools decide whether or not they want to interview you within a month.

- If you have applied to one of those medical schools that do not interview A level candidates, the next communication you receive may be a notification from UCAS that you have been made a conditional offer.
- If one or more of the medical schools decides to interview you, your next letter will be an invitation to visit the school and attend an interview. (For advice on how to prepare for the interview, see Chapter 3.)
- If you are unlucky, the next correspondence you get from UCAS will contain the news that you have been rejected by one or more of your chosen schools. Does a rejection mean it's time to relax on the A level work and dust off alternative plans? Should you be reading up on exactly what the four-year course in road resurfacing involves? No, you should not!

A rejection is a setback and it does make the path into medicine that bit steeper, but it isn't an excuse to give up. A rejection should act as a spur to work even harder because the grades you achieve at A level are now even more important. Don't give up and do turn to page 102 to see what to do when you get your A level results.

Answers to UKCAT sample questions on pages 29–32: A, C, A, A

Answer to BMAT sample question on page 33: C.

3 | The interview process

It's always difficult imagining what an interview is going to be like. However, this doesn't mean that you shouldn't prepare. While it's very important to be natural, to ensure you don't reel off a list of pre-learned answers, you can still make sure you're prepared for some general questions and that you're able to give clear, well-worded answers and to act with real confidence.

Making your interview a success

If you are lucky enough to get an interview, you need to prepare thoroughly for it, as you will not be given a second chance if you do not perform well. As with most other activities, the more you practise, the better your chance of success. Interviews can be stressful and you will be nervous, and so practice interviews are an important part of your preparation.

In this chapter, we look at many of the common types of interview question and provide you with suggestions about how to approach them. We also give you advice on how to maintain some control over the interview and how to steer it to your strengths. You can then practise using the list of sample interview questions.

The questions that we look at in this chapter have all been asked at medical school interviews over recent years, and they have been provided by students who have been interviewed and by members of a number of medical school interview panels. You cannot prepare for the odd, unpredictable questions, but the interviewers are not trying to catch you out, and they can be relied on to ask some of the general questions that are discussed here.

For most questions, there are no 'correct' answers (but there are numerous 'incorrect' answers!) and, even if there were, you shouldn't try to memorise them and repeat them as you would lines in a theatre script. The purpose of presenting these questions, and some strategies for answering them, is to help you think about your answers before the interview and to enable you to put forward your own views clearly and with confidence.

When you have read through this section, and thought about the questions, arrange for someone to sit down with you and take you through the mock interview questions. (If you have the facilities, you will find it helpful to record the interview on video, for later analysis.) You might be interested in the views of four medical professionals, quoted in the *Student BMJ*, on the qualities that they look for. These views will not have changed; in fact, time and time again they are emphasised by professionals in this field.

> *'An understanding about what being a good doctor entails from both the profession's point of view and the patient's point of view; a significant, meaningful experience of working in a healthcare environment or with disabled or disadvantaged people; an understanding of the importance of research in medicine; an awareness of the ethical issues associated with medical research; good oral communication skills and evidence of flexible and critical thinking.'*
>
> Peter McCrorie, Director of the
> Graduate Entry Programme at St George's

> *'The innate characteristics of a good doctor are beneficence and the capacity to engage with the knowledge necessary for informed practice.'*
>
> Dr Allan Cumming, Associate Dean of
> Teaching at Edinburgh University

> *'I think that you are born with some personal qualities, such as the ability to get on with people, to empathise with their distress, to inspire confidence in others, and to carry anxiety. Such qualities are very difficult to train into a person. A good doctor also needs knowledge and the experience of implementing that knowledge.'*
>
> Mike Shooter, President of the
> Royal College of Psychiatrists

> *'A medical student needs to be bright – not least to cope with a lifetime of assimilation of new concepts and knowledge. The ability to communicate, the ability to work as part of a multi-professional team, empathy and a non-prejudicial approach are qualities that should be expected in all healthcare professionals. There is also, however, a need for diversity and a need to resist any move towards personality conformity.'*
>
> John Tooke, Dean of the Peninsula Medical School

Finally, don't forget that medical school interviewers are busy people and they do not interview for the fun of it. Neither do they set out to humiliate you. They call you for interview because they want to offer you a place – make it easy for them to do so!

Typical interview questions and how to handle them

Why do you want to become a doctor?

The question that most interviewees dread! Answers that will turn your interviewers' stomachs and may lead to rejection include the following.

- I want to heal sick people.
- My father is a doctor and I want to be like him.
- The money's good and unemployment among doctors is low.
- The careers teacher told me to apply.
- It's glamorous.
- I want to join a respected profession, so it is either this or law.

Try the question now. Most sixth-formers find it quite hard to give an answer and are often not sure why they want to be a doctor. Often the reasons are lost in the mists of time and have simply been reinforced over the years.

The interviewers will be sympathetic, but they do require an answer that sounds convincing. There are four general strategies.

The story (option A)

You tell the interesting (and true) story of how you have always been interested in medicine, how you have made an effort to find out what is involved by visiting your local hospital, working with your GP, etc. and how this long-term and deep-seated interest has now become something of a passion. (Stand by for searching questions designed to check that you know what you are talking about!)

The story (option B)

You tell the interesting (and true) story of how you, or a close relative, suffered from an illness that brought you into contact with the medical profession. This experience made you think of becoming a doctor and, since then, you have made an effort to find out what is involved . . . (as before).

The logical elimination of alternatives (option C)

In this approach you have analysed your career options and decided that you want to spend your life in a scientific environment (you have enjoyed science at school) but would find pure research too impersonal. Therefore the idea of a career that combines the excitement of scientific investigation with a great deal of human contact is attractive. Since discovering that medicine offers this combination, you have investigated it (and other alternatives) thoroughly (visits to hospitals, GPs, etc.) and have become passionately committed to your decision.

The problems with this approach are that:

- they will have heard it all before
- you will find it harder to convince them of your passion for medicine.

Fascination with people (option D)

Some applicants can honestly claim to have a real interest in people. Here's a test to see if you are one of them: you are waiting in the queue for a bus/train/supermarket checkout. Do you ignore the other people in the queue or do you start chatting to them? Win extra points if they spontaneously start chatting to you, and a bonus if, within five minutes, they have told you their life story. Applicants with this seemingly magical power to empathise with their fellow human beings do, if they have a matching interest in human biology, have a good claim to a place at medical school.

Answer with conviction

Whether you choose one of these strategies or one of your own, your answer must be well considered and convincing. Additionally, it should sound natural and not over-rehearsed. Bear in mind that most of your interviewers will be doctors, and they (hopefully) will have chosen medicine because they, like you, had a burning desire to do so. They will not expect you to be able to justify your choice by reasoned argument alone. Statements (as long as they are supported by evidence of practical research) such as 'and the more work I did at St James's, the more I realised that medicine is what I desperately want to do' are quite acceptable and far more convincing than saying 'medicine is the only career that combines science and the chance to work with people', because it isn't!

> 'We make allowances for the fact that students are going to be nervous at the interview. Indeed, if the applicant is not at all nervous I would question their desire to become a doctor. We try to relax students at the beginning by asking them questions that they are expecting, for example, why medicine? We know that this is a question that students worry about, but we also know that they have probably prepared an answer for this. After this, we ask about work experience or voluntary work because this is when we can see whether they are really serious. What we are after is evidence that the student was interested in what was going on around them, and that they gained something from the experience. It is not difficult to arrange voluntary work in some capacity, so it is what they got out of it which is important, not simply having done it.'
>
> Admissions tutor

What have you done to show your commitment to medicine and to the community?

This should tie in with your UCAS application. Your answer should demonstrate that you do have a genuine interest in helping others. Ideally, you will have a track record of regular visits to your local hospital or hospice, where you will have worked in the less attractive side of patient care (such as cleaning bedpans). Acceptable alternatives are regular visits to an elderly person to do their chores, or work with one of the charities that care for homeless people or other disadvantaged groups.

It isn't sufficient to have worked in a laboratory, out of sight of patients, or to have done so little work as to be trivial: 'I once walked around the ward of the local hospital – it was very nice.' You may find that an answer such as this leads the interviewer to ask: 'If you enjoyed working in the hospital so much, why don't you want to become a nurse?' This is a tough question. You need to indicate that, while you admire enormously the work that nurses do, you would like the challenge of diagnosis and of deciding what treatment should be given.

You also need to ask yourself why admissions tutors ask about work experience. Is it because they want you to demonstrate your commitment, or because they want to know whether you have stamina, a caring nature, communication skills and, above all, the interest necessary for a medical career? If it was simply a matter of ticking boxes, then they probably would not bother to ask you about it at the interview. They ask you questions because they want to know whether you were there in body only, or if you were genuinely engaged with what was happening around you.

Why have you applied to this medical school?

Don't say:

- it has a good reputation (all UK medical schools have good reputations)
- you have low entrance requirements
- my father studied here
- it is close to the city's nightclubs.

Some of the reasons that you might have are given below.

- **Talking to people.** You have made a thorough investigation of a number of the medical schools that you have considered, by talking to your teachers, doctors and medical students you encountered during your work experience, and current students. They have given you a good picture of what it would be like to study here and have all said that it would suit you perfectly.

- **The course.** You have read the course details and feel that it is structured in way that suits your style of study and medical interests. You like the fact that it is integrated/traditional/PBL and that students are brought into contact with patients at an early date. Another related reason might be that you are attracted by the subject-based or systems-based teaching approach.
- **The open day.** You visited a number of medical schools' open days and this one was by far the most interesting and informative. While there, you talked to current medical students. You have spoken to the admissions tutor about your particular situation and asked their advice about suitable work experience, and he or she was particularly encouraging and helpful. You feel that the general atmosphere is one you would love to be part of.

Don't forget that all UK medical schools and university departments of medicine are well equipped and offer a high standard of teaching. It is therefore perfectly reasonable to say that, while you have no specific preference at this stage, you do have a great deal to give to any school that offers you a place. This answer will inevitably lead on to: 'Well, tell us what you do have to give.' That question is discussed on page 66.

> 'We give the interviewees a questionnaire to fill in before they have their interviews. We do this because it creates more time in the interview to ask them more about themselves. Although the questionnaire is important, it is not as important as a good, confident performance in the interview itself. I want the applicants to realise that if they perform well in the interview, the questionnaire is not going to adversely affect my decision as long as it is written in reasonably good English. Conversely, a brilliantly written questionnaire is not going to get a student a place if he or she performs badly at the interview.'
>
> Admissions tutor

Questions designed to assess your knowledge of medicine

No one expects you to know all about your future career before you start at medical school, but they do expect you to have made an effort to find out something about it. If you are really interested in medicine, you will have a reasonable idea of common illnesses and diseases, and you will be aware of topical issues. The questions aimed at testing your knowledge of medicine divide into seven main areas:

1. the human body (and what can go wrong with it)
2. discussing major medical issues
3. the medical profession
4. the National Health Service and funding health
5. private medicine

6. ethical questions
7. other issues.

The human body (and what can go wrong with it)

The interviewers will expect you to be interested in medicine and to be aware of current problems and new treatments. In both cases the list is endless, but the following are some areas with which you should familiarise yourself.

Your area of interest

This is how the questions might go.

> **Interviewer:** You have written on your UCAS application that you did some work-shadowing in a radiology department and that you were particularly fascinated by the MRI scanning facilities.
>
> **Candidate:** Yes, it was fascinating.
>
> **Interviewer:** What aspect of the MRI did you find fascinating?
>
> **Candidate:** Oh, everything about it.
>
> **Interviewer:** When you saw the MRI scanner being used, what were the doctors looking for?
>
> **Candidate:** I'm not sure, but it was really fascinating.

Avoid this situation by preparing well in advance. Choose a relatively well-understood procedure, such as ultrasound scans or a body system such as the cardiovascular system. Then learn how it works and (particularly for interviews at Oxbridge) prepare for fundamental questions such as 'What is meant by myocardial infarction?' and questions about what can go wrong with the system – see below.

Your work experience

If you are able to arrange work experience in a medical environment, you will want to reference it in your personal statement, but make sure that you keep a diary and that you record not only what you saw, but also medical details of what was happening.

For example, note not only that a patient was brought into casualty but what the symptoms were, what the diagnosis was and what treatment was given. Here is an example of a bad answer.

> **Interviewer:** I notice that you spent two weeks at St James's. Tell me something about what you did there.

> **Candidate:** I spent two days in the cardiology department, three days in A&E, one day in the pathology lab, two days on an oncology ward, one and a half days in neurology and half a day in general surgical. I saw sutures, drips, lung cancer . . . [etc.].

The problem here is that the interviewers are no clearer about your suitability for a career in medicine, only that you have a good memory. This approach is referred to by some admissions tutors as 'medical tourism'. Interviewers are looking for a genuine enthusiasm for medicine. They are not going to be impressed by a long list of hospital departments, treatments or illnesses unless they can see that your experience actually meant something to you on a personal level, and that you gained insights into the profession. Here is a better answer.

> **Candidate:** I was able to spend time in a number of wards, which enabled me to see a whole range of treatments. For instance, during my two days in the cardiology department, I was able to see several newly admitted patients who might have had heart attacks. I found it particularly interesting to see how careful the doctors had to be in taking the history, so that they were not putting words into the patients' mouths about their symptoms and the type of pain they were experiencing. I was also able to watch an angioplasty being performed. I was amazed at the level of skill the surgeon demonstrated – I would love to do that myself one day.

In this type of answer, your genuine enthusiasm, good observation and respect for the profession are all apparent.

> *'One piece of advice I would give any potential interviewee is to try to guess what we, the interviewers, might be worried about in their application, and try to address this in the interview. For example, the student who had not done much voluntary work at the time the UCAS application had been submitted but who had done more since should mention this. There are many ways to do this, perhaps by responding to a question about why they want to be a doctor by saying ". . . and the recent work experience I have done at X demonstrated . . .". Another example is if a student has not written much about extracurricular activities, possibly because the school does not offer much or because the student has a part-time job. This could be brought into the conversation when responding to questions about how he or she copes with stress, or about communication skills. The interviewee needs to realise that if weak areas are not covered in the interview, then we will probably be as concerned after the interview as we were before.'*
>
> Admissions tutor

Discussing major medical issues

Keep a file of cuttings

Make sure that you read *New Scientist*, *Student BMJ* and, on a daily basis, a broadsheet newspaper that carries regular, high-quality medical reporting. The *Independent* has excellent coverage of current health issues, and the *Guardian*'s health section on Tuesdays is interesting and informative. Newspapers' websites often group articles thematically, which can save time. The Sunday broadsheets often contain comprehensive summaries of the week's top medical stories.

Fashionable illnesses or the disease du jour

At any one time, the media tend to concentrate on one or two 'fashionable' diseases. The papers fill their pages with news of the latest 'epidemic' and the general public is expected to react as if the great plague of 1665 were just round the corner. In reality, CJD and SARS resulted in very small numbers of deaths, and the same can be said of recent flu outbreaks, for example. The media encourage us to react emotionally rather than logically in matters concerning risk. They advise us to stop eating beef but not to stop driving our cars, even though around 3,000 people are killed in road accidents every year. Thus, it is good to be aware of this bias as universities may ask you at interviews why it is that despite higher death rates due to obesity or alcoholism, swine flu is getting 'all the attention'.

While these diseases tend to be trivial in terms of their effect, they are often interesting in scientific terms, and the fact that they are being discussed in the media makes it likely that they will come up at interview. The next few paragraphs discuss some examples of diseases and illnesses that have seemingly gained a certain momentum and critical mass in terms of numbers of people who are diagnosed as suffering from them and therefore have been brought into the public eye.

Chronic fatigue syndrome (CFS), also known as myalgic encephalomyelitis (ME), is characterised by long-term tiredness which does not disappear with sleep. At this time, there is no cure for CFS, and any drugs that are prescribed are done so to alleviate symptoms such as headaches rather than to treat the underlying condition.

It is estimated that around 250,000 people in the UK suffer from CFS. Around a quarter of these cases are serious enough to affect daily mobility and routine tasks. Some people simply get better over time and resume their normal lives, but others can remain affected throughout their lives. For more details, visit www.nhs.uk/Conditions.

Multiple chemical sensitivity describes allergy-like symptoms caused by exposure to a range of chemicals, including perfume, petrol or diesel fuels, smoke, and organic matter such as pollen or house dust mites. Symptoms can include breathing difficulties, itchy eyes and skin, sore throats, headaches and even memory loss. The fact that there are so many varying symptoms and stimuli for the condition has led to scepticism about the real existence of the condition.

Lyme disease is an infection caused by a tick bite. The disease has a variety of symptoms, affecting the skin, heart, joints and nervous system. It is also known as borrelia or borreliosis. The disease is caused by the *Borrelia burgdorferi* microorganism, which is present on ticks that live on deer. The symptoms of the disease, which first manifests itself as a red spot caused by the tick bite, include headaches, muscle pain and swollen lymph glands, and eventually the nervous system is affected. The symptoms may be apparent days after the tick bite, but in some cases they only present themselves months or even years later.

These diseases and illnesses have become more well-known in recent times and, as a result, have gained more media coverage. This has had the effect of causing greater concern to the general public who may have been unaware of their existence otherwise.

An interviewer could decide to ask you about a particularly 'fashionable' illness such as flu, which has been reported heavily in the media, by saying: 'Why is flu again causing so much concern, when very few people have died from it?' It is important to know something about these illnesses (see Chapter 4 for information on swine flu, MRSA and HIV/AIDS) but equally important to keep them in statistical proportion. For example, nearly 2 million people die as a result of contracting diarrhoeal infections each year, mostly the result of poor sanitation and infected water supplies, and over 5 million people die as a result of injury sustained in accidents or violence.

The big killers

Diseases affecting the circulation of the blood (including heart disease) and cancer are the main causes of death in the UK. Make sure you know the factors that contribute to them and the strategies for prevention and treatment. You can read more about this in Chapter 4.

The global picture

You may well be asked about what is happening on a global scale. You should know about the biggest killers (infectious diseases and circulatory diseases), trends in population changes, the role of the World Health Organization (WHO), and the differences in medical treatments between developed and developing countries. You can read more about this in Chapter 4.

The Human Genome Project and gene therapy

You would be wise to familiarise yourself with the sequence of developments in the field of genetic research, starting with the discovery of the double helix structure of DNA by Crick and Watson in 1953. You should find out all that you can about:

- recombinant DNA technology (gene therapy, genetic engineering)
- genetic diagnosis (of particular interest to insurance companies)
- cloning
- stem cell research
- GM crops
- genetic enhancement of livestock
- 'pharming'.

Diet, exercise and the environment

The maintenance of health on a national scale isn't simply a matter of waiting until people get ill and then rushing in with surgery or medicine to cure them. There is good evidence that illness can be prevented by a sensible diet, not smoking, taking exercise and living in a healthy environment.

In this context, a healthy environment means one where food and water are uncontaminated by bacteria and living quarters are well ventilated, warm and dry. The huge advance in health and life expectancy since the middle of the nineteenth century owes much more to these factors than to the achievements of modern medicine.

However, with unhealthy eating habits and a sedentary lifestyle becoming more prevalent, one of the biggest problems developing in the UK today is obesity. It is becoming more and more of an issue and the associated problems are costing the NHS more and more money each year. For more information on this, see Chapter 4.

TIP!

When discussing medical topics, you will sound more convincing if you learn and use the correct terminology. For example, to a doctor, a patient doesn't turn up at the surgery with earache; they present with otitis. The best sources of correct terminology are medical textbooks, some of which are quite easy to understand (see Chapter 9).

The medical profession

The typical question is: 'What makes a good doctor?' Avoid answering: 'A caring and sympathetic nature.' If these really were the crucial qualities of a good doctor, there would be little point in going to medical school. Start by stressing the importance of the aspects that can be taught and, in particular, emphasise the technical qualities that a doctor needs: the ability to carry out a thorough examination, to diagnose accurately and quickly what is wrong, and the skill to choose and organise the correct treatment.

After this comes the ability to communicate effectively and sympathetically with the patient so that he or she can understand and participate in the treatment. The most important part of communication is listening. There is an old medical adage that if you listen to the patient for long enough he or she will give you the diagnosis.

Communication skills also have an important role to play in treatment – studies have shown that some patients get better more quickly when they feel involved and part of the medical team. The best way to answer a question about what qualities are necessary to be a successful doctor is to refer to your work experience. You could say: 'The ability to react quickly. For example, when I was shadowing Dr Ferguson at the Fletcher Memorial Hospital, I witnessed a case where . . .'

The National Health Service and funding health

An application to a medical school is also an application for a job, and you should have taken the trouble to find out something about your likely future employer. You should be aware of the structure of the NHS and the role that strategic health authorities, primary care trusts and foundation trusts play. You need to know about the recent changes in the way in which doctors are trained, and the career paths that are open to medical graduates. When you are doing your work experience, you should take every opportunity to discuss the problems in the NHS with the doctors who you meet. They will be able to give you first-hand accounts of what is happening, and this is a very effective way of coping with questions on the NHS.

A typical interview question is: 'What are the main problems facing the NHS?' The most impressive way to answer this is to say something along the lines of: 'Well, when I was shadowing Dr Jones at St James's Hospital, we discussed this. In his opinion, they are . . .'

This not only demonstrates that you were using your work experience to increase your awareness of the medical profession, but it also takes the pressure off you because you are not having to come up with your own views. However, be prepared to then discuss your answer in more depth.

Private medicine

Another set of questions that needs careful thought concerns private medicine. Don't forget that many consultants have flourishing private practices and rely on private work for a major part of their income.

Equally, a number of doctors do not have the opportunity to practise privately and may resent a system that allows some consultants to earn money both within and outside the NHS.

Your best bet is to look at the philosophy behind private medicine, and you may care to argue as follows below.

Most people agree that if you are run over by a bus you should be taken to hospital and treated at the taxpayers' expense. In general, urgent

treatment for serious and life-threatening conditions should be treated by the NHS and we should all chip in to pay for it. On the other hand, most of us would agree that someone who doesn't particularly care for the shape of their nose and who wants to change it by expensive plastic surgery should pay for the operation themselves. We can't ban cosmetic operations, so we are led to accept the right of private medicine to exist.

Having established these two extremes, one is left to argue about the point where the two systems meet. Should there be a firm dividing line or a fuzzy one where both the NHS and private medicine operate?

You could also point out that private medicine should not harm the NHS. For example, the NHS has a problem of waiting lists. If 10 people are standing in a queue for a bus, everyone benefits if four of those waiting jump into a taxi – providing, of course, that they don't persuade the bus driver to drive it!

Ethical questions

Medical ethics is a fascinating area of moral philosophy. You won't be expected to answer questions on the finer points but you could be asked about the issues raised below.

A patient who refuses treatment

You could be presented with a scenario, and asked what you would do in the situation. For example, you have to inform a patient that he has cancer. Without radiotherapy and chemotherapy his life expectancy is likely to be a matter of months. The patient tells you that he or she does not wish to be treated. What would you do if you were in this situation? The first thing to remember is that the interviewer is not asking you this question because he or she wants to know what the answer to this problem is. Questions of this nature are designed to see whether you can look at problems from different angles, weigh up arguments, use your knowledge of medical issues to come to a conclusion, and produce coherent and structured answers.

TIP!

You should remember that the interviewers are not interested in your opinions, but they are interested in whether you have understood the issues. A useful approach to this type of question is to:

- explain the background to the question(s)
- consider both sides of the argument
- bring current issues or examples into your answer
- only express a personal opinion at the very end.

A good technique for answering 'What would you do if you were a doctor and. . .' questions is to start by discussing the information that you would need, or the questions that you might ask the patient. In the above example, you would ask these questions.

- How old is the patient?
- Does the patient have any other medical conditions that might affect his or her life expectancy?
- Why is the patient refusing the treatment?

The answer to these questions would then determine what you would do next. The patient could be refusing treatment for religious or moral reasons; it might simply be that he or she has heard stories about the side effects of the treatment you have recommended. One possible route would be to give him or her contact details of a suitable support group, counselling service or information centre.

A classic case is someone who refuses a life-saving blood transfusion because it contravenes his or her religious beliefs. Fair enough, you may feel, but what if, on these grounds, a parent refuses to allow a baby's life to be saved by a transfusion? Similarly, in a well-publicised legal case, a woman refused to allow a caesarean delivery of her baby. The judge ruled that the wishes of the mother could be overruled. It is worth noting that the NHS (as a representative of the state) has no right to keep a patient in hospital against his or her will unless the medical team and relatives use the powers of the Mental Health Act.

TIP!

This example illustrates an effective general technique for answering difficult moral, ethical or legal questions. The interviewers are not particularly interested in your opinion, but they are interested in whether you have understood the issues. Always demonstrate this by explaining the extreme opposing views. Only then, and in a balanced and reasonable way, give your own opinion.

Euthanasia

To answer questions on euthanasia, start by making sure that you know the following correct terminology, and the law.

- **Suicide.** The act of killing oneself intentionally.
- **Physician-assisted suicide.** This involves a doctor intentionally giving a person advice on or the means to commit suicide. It describes situations where competent people want to kill themselves but lack either the means or the ability.
- **Euthanasia.** Euthanasia is a deliberate act of omission whose primary intention is to end another's life. Literally, it means a gentle

or easy death, but it has come to signify a deliberate intervention with the intention to kill someone, often described as the 'mercy killing' of people in pain with terminal illnesses.

- **Double effect.** The principle of double effect provides the justification for the provision of medical treatment that has a negative effect, although the intention is to provide an overall positive effect. The principle permits an act that foreseeably has both good and bad effects, provided that the good effect is the reason for acting and is not caused by the bad. A common example is the provision of essential pain-relieving drugs in terminal care, at the risk of shortening life. Pain relief is the intention and outweighs the risk of shortening life.
- **Non-treatment.** Competent adults have the right to refuse any treatment, including life-prolonging procedures. The British Medical Association (BMA) does not consider valid treatment refusal by a patient to be suicide. Respecting a competent, informed patient's treatment refusal is not assisting suicide.
- **Withdrawing/withholding life-prolonging medical treatment.** Not all treatment with the potential to prolong life has to be provided in all circumstances, especially if its effect is seen as extending the dying process. Cardio-pulmonary resuscitation of a terminally ill cancer patient is an extreme example. In deciding which treatment should be offered, the expectation must be that the advantages outweigh the drawbacks for the individual patient.

Currently in the UK there is a ban on assisted suicide. This is a very contentious issue and, as you can imagine, even within the medical community opinion is divided. In short, it deliberates and questions the ethical conundrum of the right of the individual to 'die with dignity' when they so wish versus those who argue that it goes against moral and religious teaching and that it is against God's law to take a life. The nature of this ethical dilemma is central to the role of a doctor, as some would argue further that it also goes against the moral duty of a doctor, which is to prolong life instead of shortening it. The Tony Nicklinson case in March 2012 brought this law into question again and the courts found themselves in conflict with parliament, which wished the case to be struck out on the grounds that the law on murder was absolute. However, the courts ruled that there was a case to answer. They forced prosecutors to clarify the law on assisted suicide. The case was granted a hearing in the courts later in the year. However, in October, the High Court rejected the 'right to die' appeal as it was concerned that this would set a precedent for murder. Campaigners continue to fight this ruling.

As it is a controversial question, it is one that can often be asked at interviews. What must be remembered is that aside from your own beliefs, whether you do or don't support euthanasia, the de facto position in the UK is that assisted suicides are currently illegal. There is, however, a Swiss-based group, Dignitas, which to date has helped nearly 200 residents of Britain to commit suicide. This has been due to their extreme suffering, which has to be well proven and documented. Dignitas was organised in 1998 to help people with chronic diseases to die, honouring the wishes of the patient and those around them to end their suffering. There is currently nothing stopping UK nationals from travelling to Switzerland and being assisted to commit suicide, but, as the law stands, loved ones and friends may be prosecuted if they help. See Chapter 4 for more information.

So one of the key questions is: 'Could you withdraw treatment from a patient for whom the prognosis was very poor, who seemed to enjoy no quality of life and who was in great pain?' The answer to this question comes in two parts. In part one, you must recognise that a decision like this could not be taken without the benefit of full medical training and some experience, together with the advice of colleagues and the fullest consultation with the patient and his or her relations, as well as knowing your position according to the law. If, after that process, it was clear that life support should be withdrawn, then, and only then, would you take your decision. Part two involves convincing the panel that, having taken your decision, you would act on it.

Other issues

A good opening question is: 'Should smokers be treated on the NHS?' On the one hand, it is certainly true that smoking is a contributory factor in heart disease. Is it fair to expect the community as a whole to spend a great deal of money on, for example, coronary artery bypass surgery if the patient refuses to abandon behaviour that could jeopardise the long-term effectiveness of the operation? Conversely, one can argue that all citizens and certainly all taxpayers have the right to treatment irrespective of their lifestyles. Further to this, one can argue that duty paid on cigarettes adds up to more than the cost of treatment.

Another series of questions recognises the fact that there is a limit to the resources available to the NHS and highlights the tough decisions that may need to be taken. The interviewer might refer to 'rationing of healthcare'. Suppose you have resources for one operation but two critically ill patients – how do you decide which one to save? Or suppose that you can perform six hip replacement operations for the cost of one coronary artery bypass. Heart bypass operations save lives; hip replacements merely improve life. Which option should you go for?

Even more controversial issues surround surgery to change gender. Should these operations be performed when the money could be used to save, or at least prolong, life?

Events are constantly bringing fresh moral issues associated with medicine into the public arena. It is important that you read the papers and maintain an awareness of the current 'hot' issues. See Chapter 9 for further reading.

Questions aimed at finding out whether you will fit in

One of the reasons for interviewing you is to see whether you will fit successfully into both the medical school and the medical profession. The interviewers will try to find out if your views and approach to life are likely to make you an acceptable colleague in a profession that, to a great extent, depends on teamwork. This does not mean that they want to hear views identical to their own. On the contrary, they will welcome ideas that are refreshing and interesting. What they do not like to hear is arrogance, lies, bigotry or tabloid headlines.

These questions have another important purpose: to assess your ability to communicate in a friendly and effective way with strangers even when under pressure. This skill will be very important when you come to deal with patients.

You may be asked how you would deal with a minor road traffic accident. You are walking on a pavement when a cyclist is hit by the door of a car when the passenger is getting out. The cyclist immediately jumps up to confront the car passenger, and both people are very irate. You are the only person around. What do you do?

The type of answer the interviewer is looking for will include the following points.

- Try to defuse the situation; interrupt them by asking if either of them is injured. Tell them the priority is to deal with any injuries.
- Carry out basic first aid if required.
- Look out for any dangers. Is the bike in the middle of the road? Is the car door blocking any other vehicles? Is the situation safe? Should you call for help?
- Phone the emergency services if required.

Questions about your UCAS application

The personal statement section, in which you write about yourself, is a fertile area for questions; as explained earlier, you should have included some juicy morsels to attract the interviewers. The most successful interviews often revolve around some interesting or amusing topic that is fun to talk about and that makes you stand out from the crowd. The trouble is that you cannot invent such a topic – it really has to exist. Nevertheless, if you really have been involved in a campaign to save an obscure species of toad and can tell a couple of amusing stories about it (make them short), so much the better.

Even if your UCAS application seems, in retrospect, a bit dull, don't worry. Work out something interesting to say. Look at what you wrote and at all costs avoid the really major disasters; if you put that you like reading, for instance, make sure you can remember and talk intelligently about the last book you read.

Sometimes an amusing comment on your application followed up by a relaxed and articulate performance at the interview will do the trick. A good example is the comment that a student made about lasting only three days as a waitress during the summer holidays. She was able to tell a story about dropped food and dry-cleaning bills, and was offered a place. Of course, failing at a part-time job is only going to be a funny story if you are relaxed enough to make it amusing; by then you will have already proved to the interviewers that you are a strong candidate, for whom this incident was an anomaly.

Questions about your contribution to the life of the medical school

These questions can come in many forms but, once identified, they need to be tackled carefully. If you say you like social life, the selectors might worry that you won't pass your pre-clinical exams. On the other hand, if you say that you plan to spend all your time windsurfing, mountaineering or fishing, they'll see you as a loner.

The best approach is probably to say that you realise that medical school is hard work and that your main responsibility must be to pass your exams. After that, you could say that the medical school can only function as a community if the individuals involved are prepared to participate enthusiastically in as many of the extracurricular activities as possible. Above all, try to talk about communal and team activities rather than more solitary pursuits.

You may find it helpful to know that, in one London medical school, the interviewers are told to ask themselves if the candidate has made good use of the opportunities available to them, and whether they have the personal qualities and interests appropriate to student life and a subsequent career in medicine. Poor communication skills, excessive shyness or lack of enthusiasm concern them, and will be taken into account when awarding scores.

Unpredictable questions

There are two types of unpredictable question: the nice and the nasty.

Nice questions

Nice questions are usually designed to test your communication skills and to assess your personality. A typical nice question would be: 'If you won 20 million pounds on the lottery, what would you do with it?'

- **Rule 1.** Don't relax! Your answer to this question needs to be as effective and articulate as any other and, while you should appear to be relaxed, you must not let your thinking or speech become sloppy.

- **Rule 2.** A nice question could also indicate that the interviewer has decided against you and simply wants to get through the allotted time as easily as possible. If you suspect that this is the case (possibly because you have said something that you now regret), this question provides an opportunity to redeem yourself. Try to steer the questions back to gritty, medical-related topics. See the advice on pages 69–70.

In answering the above question, be very careful. Take time to think. You could approach it from a medical perspective and use the money to set up a foundation to research a particular disease or condition that means something to you. This is where background knowledge and previous reading can be brought into the interview. Talk about the disease and the point to which the current research has reached. This is a starting point for your investment and then your money could be used to develop medication, vaccinations or develop a cure or preventive measure.

Nasty questions

The 'interview nasties' are included either as a test of your reaction to pressure or in response to something you have said in answer to a previous question. Here are some examples.

- Why should we choose you rather than one of the other candidates we have interviewed today?
- How could you convince me that you would make a good doctor?

There are no right answers but there is a correct approach. Start by fixing the interviewer with a big smile, then distance the question from your own case.

Regarding the first question: there is one absolute mistake that you must not make. Never compare yourself with any other candidate. You have no real idea about the quality of the other students applying. It may well be that you think you have all the qualities required to make a first-class doctor, but so will they. They would not have made the interview stage if they did not. Concentrate on your qualities. Make sure you know which qualities you have mentioned on your personal statement. Do not just recall it word for word, and, whatever you do, do not say 'as I have written in my personal statement'. Know what you have written, be able to discuss it and use your work experience to justify your answer. You should have found out during your work experience which qualities you have or even how they have developed during it.

Make sure you practise these answers before you have an interview. Either arrange a practice interview at your school or find an institution that organises these events. The more practice you get at these sorts of questions the better you will become at providing an answer.

Another 'nasty' question – one that interviewees always fear – is being asked about something scientific or technical that they have never heard of. For example: 'What is the drug x used for?'

You are not expected to have the knowledge that a qualified doctor has and so you would only be asked this type of question if the drug in question had been in the news recently, or if you had mentioned something related to it in your personal statement. So your pre-interview preparation (making sure you are up to date with recent events and being familiar with your personal statement) will help you here.

Questions about your own academic performance

These are especially likely if you are retaking A levels (or have retaken them). The question will be: 'Why did you do so badly in your A levels?' Don't say 'I'm thick and lazy', however true you feel that is!

Another bad ploy is to blame your teachers. It is part of the unspoken freemasonry of teaching that no teacher likes to hear another teacher blamed for poor results. If, however, your teacher was absent for part of the course, it is perfectly acceptable to explain this. You should also explain any other extenuating circumstances such as illness or family problems, even if you believe them to have been included in the UCAS reference. Sadly, most applicants don't have one of these cast-iron excuses!

The best answer, if you can put your hand on your heart when you deliver it, is to say that you were so involved in other school activities (head of school, captain of cricket, rowing and athletics, chairman of the community action group and producer of the school play) that your work suffered. You can't really be blamed for getting the balance between work and your other activities a little bit skewed and, even if you don't have a really impressive list of other achievements, you should be able to construct an answer on this basis. You might also add that the setback allowed you to analyse your time management skills, and that you now feel you are much more effective in your use of time.

You may also be asked how you expect to do in your A level exams. You need to show that you are working hard, enjoying the subjects and expect to achieve at least AAB (or more probably AAA – check Table 10 on pages 152–154 for admissions policies to the different medical schools).

Your questions for the interviewers

At the end of the interview, the person chairing the panel may ask if you have any questions you would like to put to the interviewers. Bear in mind that the interviews are carefully timed, and that your attempts to impress the panel with 'clever' questions may do quite the opposite.

The golden rule is: only ask a question if you are genuinely interested in the answer (which, of course, you were unable to find during your careful reading of the prospectus and website). Some medical schools, including Keele, will not allow you to ask questions of the interviewing panel. This is mainly because interviews are timed so precisely. Questions at Keele can be asked of other staff or current students during the time you are there, but not in the interview itself.

Questions to avoid

- What is the structure of the first year of the course?
- Will I be able to live in a hall of residence?
- When will I first have contact with patients?
- Can you tell me about the intercalated BSc option?

As well as being dull questions, the answers to these will be available in the prospectus and on the website, and you will show that you have obviously not done any serious research.

Questions you could ask

- I haven't studied physics at A level. Do you think I should go through some physics textbooks before the start of the course? (This shows that you are keen, and that you want to make sure that you can cope with the course. It will give them a chance to talk about the extra course they offer for non-physicists.)
- Do you think I should try to get more work experience before the start of the course? (Again, an indication of your keenness.)
- Earlier, I couldn't answer the question you asked me on why smoking causes coronary heart disease. What is the reason? (Something that you genuinely might want to know.)
- I'm really interested in the chance to do an intercalated BSc. At what point in the course do I get to choose the subject?
- When we come to choose where we will go for our elective, how much help do we get?
- How soon will you let me know if I have been successful or not?

End by saying: 'All of my questions have been answered by the prospectus and the students who showed me around the medical school. Thank you very much for an enjoyable day.' Big smile, shake hands and say goodbye.

How to structure the interview to your advantage

Having read this far you may well be asking yourself what to do if none of the questions discussed comes up. Some of them will. Furthermore, once the interviewers have asked one of the prepared questions, you should be able to lead them on to the others. This technique is very simple, and most interviewers are prepared to go along with it because it makes their job easier. All you have to do is insert a 'signpost' at the end of each answer.

Here is an example. At the end of your answer to why you want to be a doctor you could add: 'I realise, of course, that medicine is moving through a period of exciting challenges and advances.' Now stop and give the interviewer an 'over to you – I'm ready for the next question' look. Unless he or she is really trying to throw you off balance, the next question will be: 'What do you know about these advances?' Off you go with your answer, but at the end you tack on: 'Hand in hand with these technical changes have come changes in the administration of the NHS.' With luck, you'll get a question about the NHS that you can answer and end with a 'signpost' to medical ethics.

You can, if you wish, plan the whole interview so that each answer leads to a new question. The last answer can be linked to the first question so as to form a loop. The interviewers have only to ask one of the questions in the loop and you are off on a pre-planned track.

This idea never works perfectly, but it does enable you to maximise the amount of time you spend on prepared ground – time when, with luck, you'll be making a good impression. The disadvantage, of course, in having a set of prepared answers ready is that there is a temptation to pull one out of the hat regardless of what is actually being asked. The question 'Why do you want to be a doctor?' (which you might be expecting) requires a very different answer to the question 'Was there something that started your interest in being a doctor?'

One final piece of advice on interviews: keep your answers relatively short and to the point. Nothing is more depressing than an answer that rambles on. If you get a question you haven't prepared for, pause for thought, give them your best shot in a cheerful, positive voice and then be quiet!

Mock interview questions

As explained at the beginning of the chapter, interview technique can be improved with practice. You can use this section of the book as a source of mock interview questions. Your interviewer should ask supplementary questions as appropriate.

- Why do you want to be a doctor? (Supplementary: Are you sure you know what is involved?)
- (If one of your parents is a doctor.) Presumably you chose medicine because of your father/mother?
- What will you do if you don't get an offer from any medical schools?
- What evidence is there that you can cope with stress?

- Why have you applied to this medical school?
- What do you know about the course here?
- Have you come along to an open day here?
- What have you done to demonstrate your commitment to the community?
- What makes a good doctor?
- Why do you think you would make a good doctor?
- What did the doctors you have spoken to think about medicine as a career?
- What is the standard of health like in your area?
- Why is the standard of health more varied in London/Scotland/developing countries?
- Are you interested in medical research?
- What interests you about medicine? (Follow with questions about this area.)
- What do you know about AIDS? Why is it so hard to treat?
- What is the difference between a heart attack and a stroke?
- What is the link between obesity and ill health?
- What are the implications for doctors of an ageing population?
- What problems do the elderly face?
- What treatment can doctors offer to the very old?
- What do you think of homeopathy/acupuncture?
- How does diet affect health?
- How does the environment affect health?
- It was thought that tuberculosis (TB) had been eradicated. Why do you think that the number of TB cases is now on the increase?
- What roles can computers/technology play in medicine?
- Tell me about a recent article on medicine/science that you have read. Explain it.
- What are the main causes of ill health where you live?
- What advances in medicine can we look forward to during the next 10/20/50 years?
- What do you think have been the most significant developments in medicine during the last 20/50/100 years?
- What is the biggest threat to humanity over the next 20/50 years, from a medical viewpoint?
- When was the NHS formed?
- Have the reforms of the NHS been successful?
- Should GPs/primary care groups act as fundholders?
- What do you understand by the term rationing/postcode prescribing?
- Do you think private practice by NHS consultants should be abolished?
- Who is the Secretary of State for Health? What would you do if you had to take over this role?
- Can anyone undertake cloning experiments in this country? What are the arguments for and against the cloning of humans?

- Should the UK follow the Netherlands' example and make euthanasia legal?
- Is it right that the NHS should devote resources to sex-change operations when there are long waiting lists for hip replacements?
- Suppose that you were in charge of deciding which of two critically ill babies should have a life-saving operation. Imagine that there was not enough money to operate on both. How would you decide which baby to save?
- Have you come across any examples of ethical problems associated with medicine?
- What are your main interests? (The interviewer must follow up the answer with searching questions.)
- How do you think you will be able to contribute to the life of the medical school?
- What was the last book you read? Can you sum up the story in one minute?
- What do you do in your spare time?
- What is your favourite subject at A level? What do you like about it?
- What is your least favourite subject at A level? What do you dislike about it?
- Why did you do badly in your A levels/GCSEs? (For retake candidates or those with disappointing exam results.)
- Have you any questions for us?

Points for the interviewer to assess

The following is a list of criteria that the admissions staff will be looking for when interviewing candidates to determine their suitability for the course.

- Did the candidate answer in a positive, open and friendly way, maintaining eye contact for most of the time?
- Was the candidate's posture such that you felt that he or she was alert, friendly and enthusiastic?
- Was the candidate's voice pitched correctly: neither too loud nor too soft and without traces of arrogance or complacency?
- Was the candidate free of irritating mannerisms?
- Did the candidate's performance reassure you enough not to terrify you at the prospect that he or she could be your doctor in a few years?

The panel

Most medical schools have so many candidates that they operate several interview panels in parallel. This means that your interview may not be chaired by the dean, but you will certainly have a senior member of the academic staff chairing the panel. He or she will normally be assisted by two or three others. Usually, there are representatives of the clinical and pre-clinical staff and there may be a medical student on the board too. Sometimes a local GP is invited to join the panel.

While you can expect the interviewers to be friendly, it is possible that one of them may use an aggressive approach. Don't be put off by this; it is a classic interview technique and will usually be balanced by a supportive member of the panel.

Questionnaires

A number of medical schools have introduced a written component to the interview. Some, such as Nottingham, ask for a form or an essay to be sent to them prior to the interview. Others, such as St George's and King's, give each candidate a written exercise on the day of the interview. Bear in mind that a candidate who performs well in the interview, displays the necessary academic and personal qualities and is genuinely suited to medicine is unlikely to be rejected on the basis of the written element.

Dress, posture and mannerisms

You should dress smartly for your interview, but you should also feel comfortable. You will not be able to relax if you feel over-formal. For men, a jacket with a clean shirt and tie is ideal. Women should avoid big earrings, plunging necklines and short skirts. Men should not wear earrings, white socks or loud ties, or have (visible) piercings. Avoid unconventional hairstyles: no Mohicans or skinheads.

Your aim must be to give an impression of good personal organisation and cleanliness. Make a particular point of your hair and fingernails – you never see a doctor with dirty fingernails. Always polish your shoes before an interview, as this type of detail will be noticed. Don't go in smelling strongly of aftershave, perfume or food. You will be invited to sit down, but don't fall back expansively into an armchair, cross your legs and press your fingertips together in an impersonation of Sherlock Holmes. Sit slightly forward in a way that allows you to be both comfortable and alert. Make sure that you arrive early and are well prepared for the interview.

Try to achieve eye contact with each member of the panel and, as much as possible, address your answer directly to the panel member who asked the question (glancing regularly at the others), not up in the air or to a piece of furniture. Most importantly, try to relax and enjoy the interview. This will help you to project an open, cheerful personality.

Finally, watch out for irritating mannerisms. These are easily checked if you videotape a mock interview. The interviewers will not listen to what you are saying if they are all watching to see when you are next going to scratch your left ear with your right thumb!

What happens next?

When you have left the room, the person chairing the interview panel will discuss your performance with the other members and will make a recommendation to the dean. The recommendation will be one of the following:

- accept
- discuss further/waiting list
- reject.

'Accept' means that you will receive a conditional or unconditional offer.

'Discuss further' means that you are borderline, and may or may not receive an offer, depending on the quality of the applicants seen by other interview panels. If, having been classified as 'discuss further', you have been unlucky and have received a rejection, the medical school may put you on an official or unofficial waiting list. The people on the waiting list are the first to be considered in Clearing. If you have been rejected by all of the institutions you applied to, you can go through the UCAS Extra scheme, which gives you a chance to approach other universities. Details can be found on the UCAS website.

'Reject' means that you have not been made an offer. You may be luckier at one of the other medical schools to which you have applied.

The official notification of your fate will come to you from UCAS within a few weeks of the interview. If you have been rejected it is helpful to know whether you are on the waiting list and whether or not there is any point in applying again to that medical school.

Understandably, the staff will be reluctant to talk to you about your performance, but most medical schools will discuss your application with your UCAS referee if he or she calls them to ask what advice should now be given to you. It is well worth asking your referee to make that telephone call.

4| Current issues

It is obviously impossible to know about all illnesses and issues in medicine. However, being aware of some of the issues in medicine today will be of enormous benefit, particularly if you are asked, as many candidates are, to extrapolate and elucidate on 'an issue' in an interview. Showing that you have an awareness of issues on more than a passing or superficial level demonstrates intelligence, interest and enthusiasm for medicine.

This will undoubtedly stand you in good stead next to a candidate who is either very hazy or is at worst completely unaware of a major issue in medicine. The following section illustrates, albeit briefly, some of the major issues that are currently causing debate, both in medical circles and in wider society. A little bit of awareness and knowledge can go a long way to securing and leaving a positive impression on an interview panel. This section is to be read with an eye to some of the exemplar questions given in Chapter 3.

National Health Service (NHS)

'Only the Chinese People's Liberation Army, the Wal-Mart supermarket chain and the Indian Railways directly employ more people.'

NHS website

The state of the NHS is a very topical issue, and one that has elicited a lot of negative comments from practitioners. It is a very common area of questioning by interview teams.

The National Health Service was set up in 1948 to provide healthcare free of charge at the point of delivery.

Accident and emergency services had been developed and had coped well with the demands of a population under bombardment during the Second World War. Some hospitals were ancient, wealthy, charitable institutions owning valuable assets such as property in London. These hospitals charged patients who could afford to pay and treated others without charge. Doctors often worked on the same basis. Other hospitals were owned and funded by local authorities. The system was supported by low-cost insurance schemes, which were often fully or partially funded by employers.

The problem perceived by the architects of the NHS was that poorer members of society were reluctant to seek diagnosis and treatment. By funding the system out of a national insurance scheme to which every employer and employee would contribute, the government conferred on all citizens (whether employed or not) the right to free healthcare without the stigma of charity.

The service has undergone a number of reforms since 1948, by far the most fundamental of which was introduced by the Conservative Government in 1990 (although the Coalition Government's reforms may turn out to be even more far-reaching). It is important to understand what these reforms were, why they were thought to be necessary, and what the outcome has been.

By the late 1980s it was clear to the government that the NHS could not function in the future without a substantial increase in funding. The fundamental reason for this was an expected reduction in the taxpayer's contribution, linked to an anticipated increase in demand for healthcare. Let's see why this was so.

By 1990:

- the NHS had become a victim of its own success – when the service saved the life of a patient who would normally have died, that person survived to have another illness, to receive more treatment and incur more expense for the NHS
- the number of life-prolonging procedures/treatments/drugs had increased as a result of developments in medical science
- the cost of these sophisticated procedures/treatments/drugs was high, and increasing at a rate faster than inflation
- the cost of staff had increased because, while pay rates had risen, the hours worked for that pay had fallen, and at the same time the cost of training staff in the new procedures and equipment was high
- patient expectations had grown – knowledge of the new procedures/treatments/drugs meant that patients demanded access to them without delay.

The 1990 reforms

The scheme was designed to work as follows.

Hospital trusts

Before the reforms, hospitals were operated and funded by DHAs (district health authorities). The government wanted the DHAs, and later the GPs, to become 'purchasers' and the hospitals to become 'providers' in the new health marketplace. Hospitals (or groups of hospitals) were told to form themselves into NHS trusts, which would act as independent businesses but with a number of crucial (and market-diluting) differences. They were to calculate the cost of all the treatment they offered and to price it at cost to the GP purchasers. In addition, and on the assumption that there were inefficiencies within the system that needed rooting out, they were told to reduce this cost by 3% annually.

GP fundholders

GPs were encouraged to become 'fundholders'. Historically, GPs have received money according to a formula based largely on the number and age of the patients registered with them. In addition, they were now to receive annually a sum of money (the fund) based on the cost of hospital treatment and prescribed drugs received by their patients. They were to be empowered to buy hospital treatment for their patients at the best price they could find. If they could do this at a total cost lower than the fund, they could invest the surplus in their 'practice' for the benefit of their patients. (The fundholding scheme was not designed to cover the cost of acute emergency work.)

Hospitals

The effect of the reforms was dramatic and largely unpopular. Particularly unpopular was the assertion that old hospitals in areas of low population density were not economically viable and should be closed. St Bartholomew's Hospital in the City of London was an example.

Suddenly there were winners and losers in a world that had considered itself removed from the pressures of commercial life.

The 1997 reforms

The government White Paper of 1997 (entitled *The New NHS: Modern, Dependable*) made a number of suggestions.

- The replacement of the internal market with 'integrated care'. This involved the formation of 500 primary care groups typically covering 100,000 patients – bringing together family doctors and community nurses – replacing GP fundholding, which ceased to exist in 1999, but which has made a reappearance in the 2011 reforms (see page 80).
- NHSnet. Every GP surgery and hospital would be connected via the internet – it would mean less waiting for prescriptions, quicker appointments and less delay in getting results of tests.
- New services for patients. Everyone with suspected cancer would be guaranteed an appointment with a specialist within two weeks.
- NHS Direct. A 24-hour nurse-led telephone advice and information service.
- Savings. £1 billion savings from cutting paperwork would be ploughed back into patient care.

Rationing

Any suggestion of 'rationing' healthcare causes the public great concern. The issue hit the headlines in January 1999 when Frank Dobson (then Health Secretary) announced that, because of lack of funds, the use of Viagra (an anti-impotence drug) would be rationed: the NHS would only provide Viagra for cases of impotence arising from a small number of named causes. For example, a man whose impotence was caused by diabetes could be prescribed Viagra on the NHS, whereas if the cause was kidney failure, he would have to pay for the drug privately.

The publicity surrounding Viagra alerted people to other issues, in particular rationing by age and postcode prescribing.

Rationing by age

The charity Age Concern (now Age UK) commissioned a Gallup poll that, it claimed, revealed that older people were being denied healthcare and being poorly treated in both primary and secondary care. The BMA responded by arguing that people of different ages require different patterns of treatment or referral. They cited the example of the progression of cancer, which is more rapid in younger people and often needs more aggressive radiotherapy, chemotherapy or surgery.

Postcode prescribing

Until the formation of the National Institute for Clinical Excellence (NICE) (see below) in 1999, health authorities received little guidance on what drugs and treatments to prescribe. Some well-publicised cases revealed large differences in the range of drugs and treatments available between regions (hence the term 'postcode rationing'). Beta interferon, a drug that extends the remission from multiple sclerosis (MS) in some patients, was prescribed by some health authorities but not by others, and the press highlighted cases where patients were forced to pay thousands of pounds a year to buy the drug privately, when others at an identical stage of MS, but who lived a few miles away, received the drug on the NHS.

Another well-publicised issue is that of infertility treatment (IVF). Whether or not treatment on the NHS is provided depends very much on which part of the country you live in. Across the country, about one in five infertile couples receive IVF treatment (although this figure is much higher in some areas). In February 2004 the government announced that the target would rise to four in five, and that the provision would be uniform across the country. Whilst encouraging to prospective parents, there was (of course!) a downside: at that point, infertile couples who were eligible for IVF received up to three sets of treatment, giving a one in two chance of conception. Under the new arrangements, couples will have only one set of treatment, reducing the chances of conception to one in four. After that, they have to pay for the treatment themselves.

NICE

The National Institute for Clinical Excellence (NICE) was set up as a special health authority in April 1999. In April 2005 it merged with the Health Development Agency to become the new National Institute for Health and Clinical Excellence, which is still known as NICE. Its role is to provide the NHS with guidance on individual health technologies (for instance, drugs) and treatments. In the words of the chairman of NICE, Professor Sir Michael Rawlins, 'NICE is about taking a look at what's available, identifying what works and helping the NHS to get more of what works into practice.' The government at the time acknowledged that there are variations in the quality of care available to different patients in different parts of the country, and it hoped that the guidance that NICE could provide would reduce these differences.

In a speech explaining the role of NICE, the chairman said that it has been estimated that, on average, health professionals should be reading 19 medical and scientific articles each day if they are to keep up to date – in future, they could read the NICE bulletins instead.

However, NICE has not ended the controversies surrounding new treatments, since it makes recommendations based not only on clinical effectiveness but also on cost-effectiveness – something that is very difficult to judge.

A good example of a situation where a drug can be clinically effective but not cost-effective is the case of the first drug that NICE reviewed as a new treatment for influenza, called zanamivir (Relenza). Despite a hefty publicity campaign when it was introduced, NICE advised doctors and health authorities not to prescribe the drug. NICE argued that although the clinical trials showed that, if taken within 48 hours of the onset of symptoms, the duration of flu is reduced by 24 hours, there was no evidence that it would prevent the 3,000 to 4,000 deaths a year that result from complications from flu.

In addition to Relenza, NICE has investigated the effectiveness of many treatments, including:

- hip replacement joints
- therapy for depression
- treatments for Crohn's disease
- IVF treatment (see above)
- drugs for hepatitis C
- surgery for colorectal cancer
- drugs for breast cancer (taxanes)
- drugs for brain cancer (temozolomides)

- identification and management of eating disorders such as anorexia nervosa
- laser treatment in eye surgery
- treatments for obesity
- coronary artery stents.

Full details of the results of these and other investigations can be found on the NICE website (www.nice.org.uk).

2004 reforms: foundation hospitals

NHS foundation trusts, to give them their proper title, were established to provide greater ownership and involvement of patients in their local hospitals. A board of governors is elected locally and has a large say in the running of the hospitals. Direct elections for the board of governors should (it is hoped) ensure that services are directed more closely at the local community. Hospitals have been allowed to apply for foundation trust status since April 2004. There are now 52 foundation trusts.

Figure 4 shows how the NHS used to be structured and the four main bodies. However, the January 2011 proposals would change this significantly (see below).

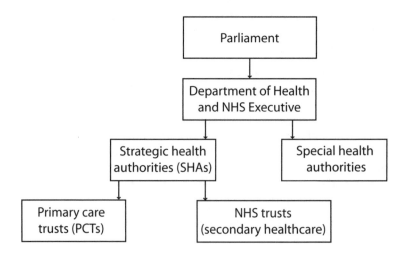

Figure 4 NHS structure pre-2011 reforms

The 2011 reforms

The then Secretary of State for Health, Andrew Lansley, released the White Paper on health reform *Equity and Excellence: Liberating the*

NHS on 12 July 2010 for implementation in 2011. (For more on this White Paper go to www.dh.gov.uk/en/Publicationsandstatistics/ Publications/PublicationsPolicyAndGuidance/DH_117353).

The main thrust of this White Paper is a shift in power that 'puts patients and their carers in charge of making decisions about their health and well-being'. The health service faces the biggest shake-up since its foundation. According to the *Financial Times*, the legislation to reform the NHS, currently being prepared by civil servants, will be far longer than the 1946 act that set up the service.

In a statement in January 2011, Andrew Lansley outlined details of how putting 'patients and their carers in charge of making decisions' would be achieved. An £80 billion budget would be devolved to around 500 GP consortiums who would in turn buy services such as operations or scans from hospitals and other specialists. They would have the freedom to choose who to buy the services from, including private hospitals, possibly even those that are based outside the UK. The 151 primary care trusts would be phased out. The government predicts that this will save the NHS £5 billion, although the scheme will cost £1.4 billion to set up. The changes are planned to be implemented fully by 2013.

The government has proposed to put the NHS in the hands of an independent panel that will control the flow of money to the GP consortiums and monitor the quality of treatment and services.

On 24 November 2011, the Department of Health published *The Operating Framework for the NHS in England 2012/13*. This has been published to help the NHS move towards the system envisaged in the White Paper mentioned above. It outlines the processes required to maintain and improve the quality of the service provided over the next few years. Not only does it refer to the standards of care required but also to the plans for financial aspects and how these can be dealt with to enable the system to run more efficiently. It states that the four main themes proposed to allow the changes to progress are:

- putting patients at the centre of decision-making in preparing for an outcomes approach to service delivery, while improving dignity and service to patients and meeting essential standards of care
- completion of the last year of transition to the new system, building the capacity of emerging clinical commissioning groups and supporting the establishment of health and well-being boards so that they become key drivers of improvement across the NHS
- increasing the pace of delivery of the quality, innovation, productivity and prevention challenge
- maintaining a strong grip on service and financial performance, including ensuring that the right to treatment within 18 weeks as set out in the NHS Constitution is met.

The Operating Framework for the NHS in England 2012/13, published by the Department of Health on 24 November 2011, can be found at www. dh.gov.uk/prod_consum_dh/groups/dh_digitalassets/documents/ digitalasset/dh_131428.pdf.

Current organisation and structure

The NHS currently consists of:

- **strategic health authorities (SHAs):** in charge of planning the healthcare for their regions
- **primary care trusts (PCTs):** providing primary care services, such as GPs, dentists, pharmacists and district nurses
- **NHS trusts:** providing secondary care (including hospitals and ambulances)
- **special health authorities:** providing services nationally, such as NHS Blood and Transplant and NICE.

NHS spending

- Under the Labour Government, the chancellor, Alistair Darling, announced a 4% a year rise for the NHS for three years – from £90 billion in 2009 to £110 billion in 2010. The Coalition Government pledged to adhere to this. However, they have been accused of breaking this as the current figure is £104 billion for spending in 2012.
- In the past five years, the NHS's spending on drugs has increased by almost 50% to £8 billion.
- Much of the increase in NHS funding has been spent on the workforce. GP and consultant pay is now among the highest in Europe, and it is estimated that about 60% of the NHS budget is spent on staffing.
- The NHS employs 300,000 more staff now than it did in 1996. This has had the effect of reducing waiting lists and waiting times significantly (at least on paper).

The NHS in 2012

The problem with this chapter is that it could be a book in itself. At the time of going to print, the NHS is in the news again as it is having to deal with a growing number of complaints within healthcare. Therefore, below are the most relevant news stories at the time of going to press.

Future structure of the NHS

The coalition has been accused of breaking all its promises over the NHS. More than 14 months after having been presented to the House of Commons, the government's plans to reform the structure of the NHS gained royal approval. The new structure is designed to make the NHS more efficient and to make savings. Figure 5 shows how the future NHS will now look.

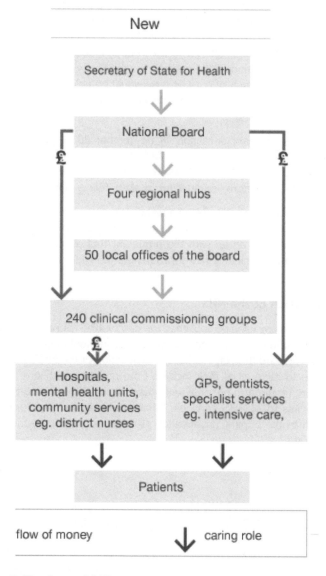

Figure 5 The future NHS
Source: http:www.bbc.co.uk/news/health-12177084.

The main idea is to address spending, as costs in the NHS have been rising for the past few years. These include the measures listed below. It will ultimately result in redundancies, with figures quoted up to £1 billion, although the government argues that any cost incurred will be small compared with the £5 billion it estimates it will save by 2015.

Closure of departments

In July 2012, Professor Terence Stephenson, the new chair of the Academy of Medical Royal Colleges (AoMRC), stated that many hospitals needed to close in order for there to be improvements within the NHS. He wanted ministers to downgrade NHS hospitals and rationalise intensive care units so as not to be 'wasteful' of NHS resources. He argued that by spreading themselves too thinly, doctors are not able to give the same amount of care as they would be able to do if they were focused in one place. His arguments were designed to implement centralisation of resources.

There is also a financial reason. In September 2012, proposals were put forward to close four London A&E departments in order to plug a £332 million gap by 2014–15. The cash flow crisis within the NHS is taking its toll and more hospitals are likely to follow suit.

While the aim is to rescue failing healthcare systems, mass protests are ongoing at various hospitals to stop the closure of critical departments; protestors do not agree with the argument that a successful department needs to be closed in order to benefit the wider area.

Privatisation of the NHS

In 2012, Andrew Lansley abolished the cap of 49% for private work that hospitals were allowed to do in order to secure additional funding. This has now opened the way for 100% privatisation of the NHS with hospitals able to raise all of their income from private healthcare. All NHS trusts are required to become self-governing by 2014 and so this measure applies to all NHS services. It has put increased pressure on the coalition as the original privatisation plans were blocked by the Liberal Democrats.

Wage freezes

Approximately 70% of the NHS trusts' budgets is spent on pay. It is expected that NHS employers will ask for a pay freeze for a third year in order to protect services. The projected savings from the pay freeze from April 2011 to March 2013 was £3.3 billion. This is expected to add to existing tensions, and trade unions warn that the NHS is losing staff over these pay conditions.

Baby boom

It was reported that NHS maternity wards are struggling, as 20,000 more babies were expected to be born in 2012. Birth rates have risen throughout the past decade and many people say that this is a result of immigration. If the number of babies reaches over 700,000 in that year, it will be the first time this has happened since 1971. This is putting a strain on midwives, prompting the Royal College of Midwives to express concerns about safety. The College also points to the shortage of midwives, which David Cameron had pledged to address at the last election, by introducing 3,000 new midwives into the profession. To date, only 900 have been delivered, so to speak.

Swine flu

As with the 'bird flu' scare in 2005 and 2006, the medical headlines in 2009 were dominated by the 'swine flu' (H1N1) pandemic. H1N1 was a new virus, containing genes from a number of viruses (human and animal), and so more people were affected than is normally the case for 'seasonal flu' since there is less natural immunity to a new virus.

Governments throughout the world tackled the problem in different ways – Mexico, for example, closed public buildings. Many countries embarked on a programme of vaccinations targeting the 'at-risk' groups: pregnant women, young children, and patients with respiratory and other problems.

The vaccines contain either live or dead viruses, and are administered either through injections or nasally. Antiviral drugs (zanamivir and oseltamivir) are used to treat patients who have contracted the illness.

The H1N1 pandemic has raised a number of questions (some of which have been discussed in recent medical school interviews).

- Demand for the vaccine outstrips supplies in many countries, which means that governments have to decide how, and to whom, the vaccine is made available. In some countries, there is an increasingly active black market trade in the vaccine, meaning that those who can afford it and who are willing to buy it directly are able to get the vaccine, whereas poorer people cannot.
- Many governments (including the UK) launched large-scale publicity campaigns soon after H1N1 was identified as being a threat, raising (some might argue) unnecessary concerns among the population, which in turn put extra pressures on already stretched health service resources.
- Public reaction to the condition was arguably more extreme, given that the virus was publicised as being 'swine flu' rather than H1N1 or another seasonal flu. The same happened with 'bird flu' two years earlier.

In July 2009, the UK government's Chief Medical Officer was predicting a minimum of 3,000 deaths in the UK, and mentioned an upper limit of 65,000. However, the actual number of deaths was around 500. As a result, the public has become more sceptical about warnings of pandemics. Nevertheless, flu continues to cause deaths, and in the winter of 2010–11 around 350 people in the UK had died as a result of the illness by the end of January 2011 (around 75% of the deaths were attributed to swine flu, the rest to other strains of flu). The 2011–12 flu season was the mildest on record according to the Health Protection Agency (HPA), with a drop in the number of hospitalisations and deaths in intensive care. The H1N1 swine flu strain is one of the main viruses that will be circulating during the winter of 2012–13 and has been included in the seasonal flu vaccine.

There is a new strain of swine flu developing in the USA that has affected 250 people since its existence was discovered in August 2011. The strain of H3N2 is different from the seasonal flu virus. There are no cases of H3N2 in the UK or in Europe, so the risk to people over here is extremely low.

For current information, visit the WHO's Global Alert and Response pages at www.who.int/csr.

MRSA and *Clostridium difficile*

Ten years ago, most people had not heard of methicillin-resistant *Staphylococcus aureus* (MRSA). Now, horror stories abound (not all of them true) of people going into hospital to have an ingrowing toenail treated, and having to stay for six months due to picking up an MRSA infection while there. It is estimated that 100,000 people each year catch the infection in UK hospitals, and that 5,000 of them die from it. The true extent of the problem is not really known. This is not to say that there is any form of cover-up; it is simply that many people who are infected with MRSA in hospitals die from causes associated with the conditions that caused them to be in hospital in the first place.

The rate of infection in the UK is one of the highest in the world because of poor hygiene in hospitals. The infection spreads via staff who handle different patients throughout the day without washing their hands in between contact with one patient and the next, or because hospital wards are not cleaned properly. If the organisms that cause MRSA get into the blood system of people weakened by illness or age, through a wound or an injection, the effects can be very serious. Since the organism is resistant to many antibiotics, it is extremely difficult to treat.

In December 2004, the *Independent* reported that the NHS was spending more than £1 billion a year in trying to prevent and treat the disease, and that over the previous seven years the number of deaths from MRSA had doubled.

There were around 2,500 deaths attributed to *Clostridium difficile* (*C. difficile*), another hospital-acquired infection, reported in 2008, a 29% decrease from 2007.

This is obviously a real problem for doctors and the medical profession as a whole. Because of this it is often a point of discussion at interview. The following questions have been asked to candidates over the last few years.

- Why are there not accurate figures about the numbers of deaths caused by MRSA and *C. difficile*?
- What is being done to try to prevent infections?
- Why might the organisms be resistant to antibiotics?
- Why are death rates now falling?

More recently (November 2011), another report in the *Independent* stated that medical experts are warning that the world is being forced into an 'unthinkable scenario of untreatable infections'. A species of bacteria called *Klebsiella pneumoniae* (*K. pneumoniae*), known to cause urinary and respiratory diseases, has been shown to be responsible for up to 50% of blood poisoning cases in some European countries. This is particularly worrying as over the last few years these bacteria have become more and more resistant to antibiotics, even to a group of drugs called carbapenems. These are often used as the last line of defence against multiple-resistant bacteria.

In the UK, more than 70 patients have been found to have bacteria living in their intestines containing a gene called NBM-1. This gene causes the production of an enzyme that breaks down carbapenems and renders the antibiotic useless. If this type of bacteria spreads, which is probable without effective drugs, this will be problematic and costly for the NHS. The UK HPA has this year warned doctors that the drugs commonly used to treat gonorrhoea are no longer effective and that a combination of drugs should be used. Without combined drug therapy, there is a possibility that a disease as common as gonorrhoea will be untreatable in the near future.

In 2012, the *Guardian* published an article reporting that the number of deaths from the MRSA superbug have fallen for a fourth successive year. Last year's figures show that 364 people died in 2011 compared with 485 in 2010, reflecting a 25% fall. The number of deaths from *C. difficile* also dropped, from 2,704 to 2,053. The hope is that these deaths continue to drop for a fifth year.

This is the sort of information you should be aware of when preparing yourself for interview.

Cervical cancer

Cancer of the cervix is a relatively rare type of cancer. However, it is the second most common cancer in women aged under 35, after breast cancer. In the UK, around 3,500 women are diagnosed with it each year.

This has been brought to our consciousness by the death of Jade Goody, a *Big Brother* celebrity, in 2009.

The symptoms of cervical cancer are not always obvious. It may not cause any symptoms at all until it has reached an advanced stage. If cervical cancer causes symptoms, the most common is abnormal vaginal bleeding, such as between periods or after sexual intercourse.

The cervix is the lower part (or neck) of the womb. It is made of muscle tissue and is the entrance to the womb from the vagina, and it can be affected by two main types of cervical cancer.

- Squamous cell carcinoma is the most common type of cervical cancer. It develops from the squamous cells, which are the flat cells in the outer layer of the cervix at the top of the vagina.
- Adenocarcinoma develops from the cells that line the glands in the cervix. Adenocarcinoma can be more difficult to detect using cervical screening tests.

Cause

This type of cancer (as well as some throat cancers, due to the practice of unsafe oral sex) is caused by HPV, which stands for human papilloma viruses. Genital HPV is usually spread through intimate, skin-to-skin contact during sex and affects the skin and the moist membranes that line parts of the body, including:

- the cervix
- the anus
- the lining of the mouth and throat.

In September 2008, the NHS launched a vaccination programme for HPV. The vaccine provides protection against the two types of HPV that cause cervical cancer.

The prognosis is good if the cancer is caught early: early-stage cancer that is confined to the cervix can usually be successfully treated through surgery and/or radiotherapy. Also, cervical cancer can be prevented from developing if it is detected in the early stages via cervical screening, but in 2012 it was reported that one in five women are still missing their cervical cancer screenings. As reported by Cancer Research UK, women in deprived areas are at higher risk of both developing and dying from cervical cancer.

However, if the cancer has spread to the surrounding areas, such as the vagina, bladder or lymph nodes, the outlook is less positive.

For more information visit www.cancerhelp.org.uk/about-cancer/cancer-questions/what-is-the-hpv-virus and www.macmillan.org.uk/Cancerinformation/Cancertypes/Cervix/Cervicalcancer.aspx.

Obesity

Obesity is an increasing problem throughout the UK, especially in the younger generation. The latest Health Survey for England reveals that about 26.1% of adults and 16% of children are clinically obese. The government predicts that if measures are not taken soon, by the year 2050 60% of the men in Britain will be obese, 50% of women and 25% of children. Obesity is defined as having a body mass index (BMI) of above 30.

The main causes of obesity are a combination of a lack of exercise and the consumption of excessive calories. Obesity has detrimental effects on many components of the human body, especially in later life. The extra body weight means the heart has to work harder and therefore there is an increase in blood pressure: this can lead to coronary heart disease. Atherosclerosis often occurs, which is a build-up of cholesterol and fatty substances in the lining of the arteries. This reduces the flow of blood and therefore oxygen to the heart muscle or other tissues such as the brain. Without oxygen even for a short time, these cells die and cease functioning. Obesity has also been shown, among other conditions, to cause respiratory problems, type 2 diabetes and osteoarthritis due to the extra strain on the joints. The government produced a White Paper called *Healthy Lives, Healthy People: Our strategy for public health in England*. This paper, along with a document produced by the Department of Health, sets out how the problem of obesity will be dealt with over the coming years. Visit www.dh.gov.uk/en/Publicationsand-statistics/Publications/PublicationsPolicyAndGuidance/DH_121941 for more details.

World health

In an interview you should be able to discuss possible reasons for the changes in death rates from causes such as cancer and heart problems, and for the difference in mortality rates between men and women.

A third area that may generate questions in interviews is the state of medicine and healthcare in less economically developed countries (LEDCs). The nature of diseases and causes of death in poor countries are very different from those in the West.

Therefore, an understanding of the major water-borne diseases, such as cholera, and contagious diseases such as smallpox and/or leprosy is of value. In addition, many of these countries have the extra burden that comes with improving incomes and life expectancies: the number of lifestyle diseases, such as cancer, is on the increase.

Rich versus poor

The world population is about 7 billion and growing. The biggest killers are infectious diseases (28 million since 1981) such as AIDS, malaria and tuberculosis, and circulatory diseases (17 million per year) such as coronary heart disease and stroke. According to the latest figures, cancer kills about 7.6 million people every year.

Infectious diseases that were once thought to be under control, such as tuberculosis, cholera and yellow fever, have made a comeback. This is due, in part, to the increasing resistance of certain bacteria to antibiotics. The antibiotics that we use now are essentially modifications to drugs that have been in use for the past 30 or 40 years, and random genetic mutations allow resistant strains to multiply.

The current global economic recession

As a consequence of the financial crisis in Organisation for Economic Co-operation and Development (OECD) countries, the world is suffering the most serious economic downturn since the 1930s. According to the WHO, this recession is having significant and detrimental effects on the ability of countries and communities to establish a good healthcare system. The impact of earlier increases in the cost of food and fuel are estimated to have tipped more than 100 million people back into poverty. The challenge facing the world now is to prevent an economic crisis becoming a social and a health crisis.

The WHO highlights concerns about some of the countries that face particular risks, including those that have high debts and whose potential spending is affected by loan repayments, islands that may be affected by rising sea levels due to global warming, and countries that are (or have recently been) involved in conflicts with neighbours.

Earlier economic crises in the 1980s and 1990s started in developing countries, and this lack of focus could result in more future pandemics. The global community has to spend to ensure that this does not occur. The long-term cost of inaction, especially on the part of the wealthy nations, could prove to be disastrous.

The effects of an ageing population

Life expectancy continues to rise (except in many sub-Saharan African countries, which have been ravaged by HIV/AIDS) because of improvements in sanitation and medical care. According to the WHO, the number of people aged 60 or over will more than triple by 2050, from about 600 million now to 2 billion. Within five years it is expected that the number of adults over 65 will outnumber children under the age of five. Birth rates in most countries are falling, and the combination of the two brings considerable problems. The relative number of people who succumb to chronic illness (such as cancer, diabetes or diseases of the circulatory system) is increasing, and this puts greater strain on countries' healthcare systems.

A useful indicator is the dependency ratio – the percentage of the population that is economically dependent on the active age group. It is calculated as the sum of 0- to 14-year-olds and over-65s divided by the number of people aged between 15 and 59. This ratio is rising steadily. The WHO website contains data for each country (www.who.int).

That said, there is a new baby boom in the UK, and that is introducing new strains of its own on the healthcare system (see page 84).

Infectious diseases

In the industrialised world, infectious diseases are well under control. The main threats to health are circulatory diseases (such as heart disease and stroke), cancer, respiratory ailments and musculoskeletal conditions (rheumatic diseases and osteoporosis). All of these are diseases that tend to affect older people and, as life expectancy is increasing, they will become more prevalent in the future. Many are nutrition-related, where an unhealthy diet rich in saturated fats and processed foods leads to poor health.

In poorer countries, infectious diseases such as malaria, cholera, tuberculosis, hepatitis and HIV/AIDS are much more common. Malaria affects up to 250 million people a year and kills about 655,000, and 1.5 million die from tuberculosis. The United Nations (UN) estimated that in 2012, 2.5 million people were newly infected with HIV/AIDS and 1.7 million people died from AIDS-related causes. Currently, 34.2 million people in the world are living with HIV.

Infectious diseases go hand in hand with poverty: overcrowding, lack of clean water and poor sanitation all encourage the spread of disease, and lack of money reduces access to drugs and treatment. The WHO estimates that nearly 2 million deaths worldwide each year are attributable to unsafe water and poor sanitation and hygiene.

In its report on infectious diseases published in 2000, the WHO highlighted the problem of antimicrobial resistance. Although antimicrobial resistance is a natural phenomenon, the result of genetic mutation and 'survival of the fittest', the effect has been amplified in recent years by the misuse of antimicrobials. Many treatments that were effective 10 years ago are no longer so, and it is a sobering thought that there have been no major new developments in antimicrobial drugs for 30 years. Given that new drugs take at least 10 years to develop and test, it is easy to see that a problem is looming. The WHO's former director-general, Dr Gro Harlem Brundtland, was quoted in the health pages of the CNN website (www. edition.cnn.com/HEALTH) as saying: 'We currently have effective medicines to cure almost every infectious disease, but we risk losing these valuable drugs and our opportunity to control infectious diseases.'

Although it is commonly stated that the overuse of antimicrobials is the cause of the problem, it might be argued that it is actually their underuse that has done the damage, since it is the pathogens that survive that cause the resistance.

Tourism also plays a part in the spread of diseases. The number of cases of malaria, yellow fever and other infectious diseases in developed countries is increasing as tourists catch the infections prior to returning to their own countries.

Life expectancy

Life expectancy figures for selected countries are shown in Table 7. These figures could be the source of many interview questions, such as the ones listed below.

Information taken from the BBC News website: www.bbc.co.uk/news/world.

- Why does Japan have the highest life expectancy?
- Why does France have a higher life expectancy than the UK?
- Why is the healthy life expectancy (HALE) in Afghanistan low?
- Why are most of the countries with the lowest HALE figures located in the middle and southern parts of Africa?

You can probably guess the answers to these, but, if not, further data is available at www.who.int/gho/en.

Table 7 Life expectancy figures for selected countries

Country	Life expectancy (years)
Japan	83
France	81
UK	80
USA	78
Zimbabwe	51
Angola	51
Sierra Leone	49
Zambia	48

Information taken from the BBC News website: www.bbc.co.uk/news/world

HIV/AIDS

To date, about 75 million people have become infected since the disease was first recognised in 1981, and 32 million have died. The number of new infections and deaths is slowing down globally as a result of improved education and the wider availability of treatments. The number of people with HIV who received antiretroviral (ARV) treatment in 2008 was about 4 million (although the WHO estimates that there are a further 9.5 million people who require ARV therapy). In the worst affected continent, Africa, there is a decline in the number of new infections of up to 25% in six countries within the 15 to 24 age group. This goes hand in hand with a decline in the rate of sex among young people and the increased use of condoms. However, in some parts of the world, such as eastern Europe and central Asia, the number of new infections continues to rise. In contrast, the number of people living with HIV/AIDS is increasing, thanks to the effectiveness of ARV therapies.

Table 8 shows regional statistics for HIV and AIDS for 2010. These statistics on the world epidemic of AIDS and HIV were published by UNAIDS/WHO in December 2011.Table 9 shows the global summary of the AIDS epidemic published in 2012.

Table 8 Regional statistics for HIV and AIDS for 2010

Region	Adults and children living with HIV/AIDS	Adults and children newly infected	Adult prevalence	AIDS-related deaths in adults and children
Sub-Saharan Africa	22,900,000	1,900,000	5.0%	1,200,000
Middle East and North Africa	470,000	59,000	0.2%	35,000
South and South-east Asia	4,000,000	270,000	0.3%	250,000
East Asia	790,000	88,000	0.1%	56,000
Oceania	54,000	3,300	0.3%	1,600
Latin America	1,500,000	100,000	0.4%	67,000
Caribbean	200,000	12,000	0.9%	9,000
Eastern Europe and Central Asia	1,500,000	160,000	0.9%	90,000
Western and Central Europe	840,000	30,000	0.2%	9,900
North America	1,300,000	58,000	0.6%	20,000

Taken from WHO and UN AIDS report on Global HIV/AIDs Response 2011.

Some of you might have noticed that the figures in this table are significantly different from earlier statistics. This is because the WHO revised its estimates last year after adopting improved information collecting and surveillance methods. The WHO's current estimate of about 34.2 million people living with HIV replaces the 2006 estimate of nearly 40 million. It is estimated that only one in 10 of the people who are infected with HIV or AIDS is aware of the fact. In regions where ARV

Table 9 Global summary of the AIDS epidemic in 2011

	Total	Adults	Children (under 15 years old)
Number of people living with HIV	34,200,000	30,700,000	3,400,000
People newly infected with HIV in 2011	2,500,000	2,200,000	330,000
AIDS deaths in 2011	1,700,000	1,500,000	230,000

Source: www.who.int/hiv/data/2012_epi_core_en.png.

therapy is freely available, there is a significant increase in the number of people who are prepared to undergo HIV/AIDS testing. This has the effect of raising awareness, which in turn reduces the stigma and encourages people to discuss and to confront the disease. This is an important factor in reducing the rate of infection.

It is clear that the only effective way of tackling HIV/AIDS is to adopt sustained and comprehensive programmes in affected areas; short-term measures or individual charities working in isolation have little chance of making a significant impact. The WHO has identified some of the elements that are important in an AIDS/HIV programme as:

- availability of cheap (or free) male and female condoms
- availability of free ARV therapy
- availability of effective and free treatment of all sexually transmitted diseases
- education programmes
- clear policies on human rights and effective antidiscrimination legislation
- willingness on the part of national governments to take the lead in the programme.

Currently there are 21 vaccines undergoing trials.

Women and AIDS

In some sub-Saharan African countries more than 75% of young people living with HIV/AIDS are women, and in the sub-Saharan region as a whole the rate of infection among women in the 15 to 24 age group is over three times greater than that among males in the same age group. Yet surveys in parts of Zimbabwe and South Africa indicate that nearly 70% of women have only ever had one sexual partner, and education programmes targeting women have been relatively effective. The main cause of the spread of the infection in Africa (and increasingly in India and south-east Asia) is through men having unprotected sex with sex workers and subsequently passing on the disease to their partners. This, in turn, increases the incidence of mother-to-baby infection.

Natural disasters

In the past couple of years, the landslides in Brazil, the floods in Sri Lanka, and the earthquake in Haiti have tended to focus the world's attention on the devastation caused by a natural disaster, particularly if it happens in the less developed world. However, don't forget that developed nations are also affected – for example, the severe flooding in Queensland followed by Cyclone Yasi in Australia in early 2011 or the devastation on the east coast of America after Superstorm Sandy in 2012.

Whenever a natural disaster occurs (floods, earthquakes or other events that displace people from their homes), food supplies are affected and clean water supplies are contaminated, which results in an enormous increase in infectious diseases such as diarrhoea, cholera and typhoid. In addition, malnutrition and difficulties in providing adequate medical treatment contribute to the number of deaths. Obviously, Western nations can cope with these emergencies much better than poor ones.

The earthquake in Pakistan in October 2005 killed 73,000 people, left another 70,000 injured and made 3 million homeless. As well as the problems associated with a lack of clean drinking water, it is estimated that in the three months following the earthquake, 13,000 women delivered babies and many of these mothers and their children needed immediate medical attention.

Even the world's richest and most powerful country, the US, was unable to cope with the aftermath of Hurricane Katrina, which hit the Gulf of Mexico in August 2005 and killed over 1,300 people, leaving a further 375,000 homeless. Superstorm Sandy killed 110 people and left thousands more homeless, with $50 billion worth of damage caused across the affected areas of the US. Disasters with human causes, particularly wars and persecution of ethnic groups, also cause people to be displaced from their homes, and many of the same problems caused by natural disasters are prevalent.

Moral and ethical issues

Lastly, the weighted and complex questions that have a moral and/or ethical dimension constitute a very relevant and current area that has caused large amounts of discussion – and, indeed, can often polarise opinion. Many medical students with whom I have spoken tell me that, almost without exception, either one or several of the following issues were discussed at the interview stage.

Genes: medical and ethical issues

Many illnesses are thought to be caused by defective genes: examples are cancer, cystic fibrosis and Alzheimer's disease. The defects may be hereditary or can be triggered by external factors such as ionising or solar radiation. The much-hyped dream of medical researchers, especially in the US, is that the affected chromosomes could be repaired, allowing the body to heal itself.

To make this dream come true, scientists need to discover which gene is causing the problem and work out how to replace it with a healthy one. Great progress has been made in solving the first part of the puzzle, thanks to a gigantic international research project known as the Human Genome Project, which has as its aim the identification of every human gene and an understanding of what effect it has. The full sequence was published in early 2000. Many links have been made between diseases and specific genes, but the techniques for replacing the defective genes have yet to prove themselves effective.

Two methods have been proposed.

1. The healthy gene is incorporated into a retrovirus which, by its nature, splices its genetic material into the chromosomes of the host cell. The virus must first be treated in order to prevent it causing problems of its own. This 'denaturing' reduces the positive effects and, to date, the trials have been unconvincing.
2. The healthy gene is incorporated into a fatty droplet, which is sprayed into the nose in order to reach cells in the lining of the nose, air passages and lungs, or injected into the blood. It was hoped that this method would be effective against the single defective gene that causes cystic fibrosis but, again, the trials have yet to prove successful.

To make matters more complicated, it turns out that many of the illnesses that are genetic in origin are caused by defects in a wide number of genes, so the hoped-for magic bullet needs to be replaced by a magic cluster bomb – and that sounds suspiciously like the approach used by conventional pharmaceuticals. Since 1990, when gene therapy for humans began, about 300 clinical trials (involving diseases ranging from cystic fibrosis and heart disease to brain tumours) have been carried out, with very limited success.

Genetic engineering

Genetic engineering is the name given to the manipulation of genes. There is a subtle difference between genetic engineering and gene therapy: specifically, that genetic engineering implies modification of the genes involved in reproduction. These modifications will then be carried over into future generations.

One of the reasons for considering these ideas is to try to produce enhanced performance in animals and plants. The possibility of applying genetic engineering to humans poses major ethical problems and, at present, experiments involving reproductive cells are prohibited. Nevertheless, one form of genetic engineering known as genetic screening is allowed. In this technique, an egg is fertilised in a test tube. When the embryo is two days old, one cell is removed and the chromosomes are tested to establish the sex and presence of gene defects. In the light of the tests, the parents decide whether or not to implant the embryo into the mother's womb.

Taken to its logical conclusion, this is the recipe for creating a breed of supermen. The superman concept may be morally acceptable when applied to racehorses, but should it be applied to merchant bankers?

How would we feel if a small, undemocratic state decided to apply this strategy to its entire population in order to obtain an economic advantage? Could we afford to ignore this challenge?

The fundamental argument against any policy that reduces variation in the human gene pool is that it is intrinsically dangerous because, in principle, it restricts the species' ability to adapt to new environmental challenges. Inability to adapt to an extreme challenge could lead to the extinction of our species.

In 2012, the Nobel prize-winning discovery of re-programming cells is offering scientists a way around the ethical issues of human embryos. Stem cells can be implanted with the source codes required to re-programme other cells within the body, acting as a control centre. This is still relatively new and presents safety as well as ethical concerns.

Euthanasia and assisted deaths

Euthanasia is illegal in the UK, and doctors who are alleged to have given a patient a lethal dose of a medication with the intention of ending that person's life have been charged with murder. UK law also prohibits assisting with suicide. The Suicide Act of 1961 decriminalised suicide in England and Wales, but assisting a suicide is a crime under that legislation.

Section 2(1) of the Suicide Act 1961 provides:

> 'A person who aids, abets, counsels or procures the suicide of another, or an attempt by another to commit suicide, shall be liable on conviction on indictment to imprisonment for a term not exceeding 14 years.'

However, in order to prove the offence of aiding and abetting it is necessary to prove firstly that the person in question had taken their own life and, secondly, that an individual or individuals had aided and abetted the person in committing suicide.

In December 2004, a High Court judge allowed a husband to take his wife (referred to as Mrs Z in the case) to Switzerland – where the law on euthanasia is different – to help her to die. Mrs Z was unable to travel alone as she had an incurable brain disease, but the local authorities had tried to prevent her husband taking her. It was reported in the *Observer* in December 2004 that an estimated 3% of GPs in the UK had helped patients to die. The *Observer* also stated that in a poll of doctors, 54% favoured legalising euthanasia. The BMA website provides detailed information on the law in a number of countries, and the ethical considerations behind euthanasia.

The debate is ongoing, and a very recent example of the conundrum that still exists is the case of the rugby player Daniel James, who in 2007 was made a tetraplegic after a rugby accident. After several attempts at suicide in the UK he was directed to Dignitas in Switzerland, where he committed suicide in 2008.

The police have investigated the acts of Daniel's parents and a family friend and concluded that there would be sufficient evidence to prosecute each of them for an offence of aiding and abetting Daniel's suicide. However, contrary to the law (see above), it was decided that, on the particular facts of this case, a prosecution would not be in the public interest. It is interesting that the police are taking this stance, but it does reflect the complexity of such ethical matters. See www.cps.gov.uk/news/articles/death_by_suicide_of_daniel_james for more information.

In another case, as reported by the BBC, in 2009 a woman with multiple sclerosis made legal history by winning her battle to have the law on assisted suicide clarified. Debbie Purdy wanted to know if her husband would be prosecuted if he helped her end her life in Switzerland. See http://news.bbc.co.uk/1/hi/8176713.stm. Five Law Lords ruled that the Director of Public Prosecutions (DPP) must specify when a person might face prosecution. Ms Purdy said that the Law Lords' decision was 'a huge step towards a more compassionate law'.

In February 2010 the DPP published its revised policy on prosecuting assisted suicide cases. The Crown Prosecution Service website gives details of the public interest factors against prosecution. These include:

1. the victim had reached a voluntary, clear, settled and informed decision to commit suicide
2. the suspect was wholly motivated by compassion

3. the actions of the suspect, although sufficient to come within the definition of the offence, were of only minor encouragement or assistance

4. the suspect had sought to dissuade the victim from taking the course of action which resulted in his or her suicide

5. the actions of the suspect may be characterised as reluctant encouragement or assistance in the face of a determined wish on the part of the victim to commit suicide

6. the suspect reported the victim's suicide to the police and fully assisted them in their enquiries into the circumstances of the suicide or the attempt and his or her part in providing encouragement or assistance.

Source: www.cps.gov.uk/publications/prosecution/assisted_ suicide_policy.html.

Writing in *The Times* on the day that the new guidelines were released, Keir Starmer, the DPP, stated:

'Assisted suicide involves assisting the victim to take his or her own life. Someone who takes the life of another undertakes a very different act and may well be liable to a charge of murder or manslaughter. That distinction is an important one that we all need to understand.

Ultimately, as many people recognised, each case is unique; each case has to be considered on its own facts and merits; and prosecutors have to make professional judgements about difficult and sensitive issues.

The assisted suicide policy will help them in that task.'

Source: www.timesonline.co.uk/tol/comment/columnists/ guest_contributors/article7039977.ece (subscription only)

More recently, the Tony Nicklinson case in March 2012 brought this law into question again. Tony Nicklinson was left paralysed from the neck down after a stroke, leaving him with 'locked-in syndrome'. While High Court judges sympathised with his case, they refused his appeal to grant immunity to a doctor to help him end his life, stating that it was for parliament to decide, not the judicial process. Even though Tony Nicklinson died of pneumonia six days after this hearing, the family continue to fight this ruling for other sufferers in similar predicaments.

You can find more information about the DPP's policy on assisted suicide at www.cps.gov.uk/publications/prosecution/assisted_suicide_ policy.html.

The internet

The internet provides the medical world with many opportunities but also some problems. The wealth of medical information available on the internet enables doctors to gain access to new research, treatments and diagnostic methods quickly. Communication between doctors, hospitals, research groups and governing bodies is simple, and news (e.g. the outbreak of a disease) can be sent around the world in a matter of minutes. The internet can also be used to create web-based administrative systems, such as online appointment booking for patients.

For patients, the internet can be used to find out about treatments for minor illnesses or injuries without having to visit a doctor or a hospital. A good site to investigate is NHS Choices (www.nhs.uk), which also provides patients with a search engine to locate local doctors.

Not all of the information available, however, is reliable. Anyone can set up a website and make it appear to be authoritative. Type 'cancer', for example, into Google and you will find nearly 2 billion sites or articles listed! Some of these are extremely useful, such as information sites provided by doctors, health organisations or support groups. However, there is also an enormous number of sites selling medicines or treatments (which in the best cases may be harmless, but could also be extremely dangerous) and quack remedies. Even if the medication that is purchased is the correct one for the condition, the drugs could be fake, of inferior quality or the incorrect dosage. In many cases, side effects from one type of medication need other drugs to control them.

The internet also allows patients to self-diagnose. The dangers of doing this range from attributing symptoms to something life-threatening (and then buying harmful drugs from another website) to gaining reassurance that the condition is harmless when it might actually be something very serious.

5| Results day

The A level results will arrive at your school on the third Thursday in August. For International Baccalaureate (IB) qualifications it will be in the first week of July and for students studying in Scotland it will be the first week of August. The medical schools will have received them a few days earlier. You must make sure that you are at home on the day the results are published. Don't wait for the school to post the results slip to you. Get the staff to tell you the news as soon as possible. If you need to act to secure a place, you may have to do so quickly. This chapter will take you through the steps you should follow – for example, you may need to use the Clearing system because you have good grades but no offer. It also explains what to do if your grades are disappointing.

What to do if things go wrong during the exams

If something happens when you are preparing for or actually taking the exams that prevents you from doing your best, you must notify both the exam board and the medical schools that have made you offers. This notification will come best from your head teacher and should include your UCAS number. Send it off at once; it is no good waiting for disappointing results and then telling everyone that you felt ghastly at the time but said nothing to anyone. Exam boards can give you special consideration if the appropriate forms are sent to them by the school, along with supporting evidence.

Your extenuating circumstances must be convincing. A 'slight sniffle' won't do! If you really are sufficiently ill to be unable to prepare for the exams or to perform effectively during them, you must consult your GP and obtain a letter describing your condition.

The other main cause of underperformance is distressing events at home. If a member of your immediate family is very seriously ill, you should explain this to your head teacher and ask him or her to write to the examiners and medical schools.

With luck, the exam board will give you the benefit of the doubt if your marks fall on a grade border. Equally, you can hope that the medical school will allow you to slip one grade below the conditional offer, although this is rare now that there are so many applicants chasing a small number of places. If things work out badly, then the fact that you declared extenuating circumstances should ensure that you are treated sympathetically when you reapply through UCAS.

The medical school admissions departments are well organised and efficient, but they are staffed by human beings. If there were extenuating circumstances that could have affected your exam performance and that were brought to their notice in June, it is a good idea to ask them to review the relevant letters shortly before the exam results are published.

What to do if you hold an offer and get the grades

If you previously received a conditional offer and your grades equal or exceed that offer, congratulations! You can relax and wait for your chosen medical school to send you joining instructions. One word of warning: you cannot assume that grades of A*AB satisfy an AAA offer. This is especially true if the B grade is in chemistry. Call your chosen university and confirm that you have met your offer.

What to do if you have good grades but no offer

Very few schools keep places open and, of those that do, most will choose to allow applicants who hold a conditional offer to slip a grade rather than dust off a reserve list of those they interviewed but didn't make an offer to. Still less are they likely to consider applicants who appear out of the blue – however high their grades. That said, it is likely that every summer a few medical schools will have enough unfilled places to consider a Clearing-style application.

If you hold three A grades but were rejected when you applied through UCAS, you need to let the medical schools know that you are out there. The best way to do this is by email. Contact details are listed in the UCAS directory. If you live nearby, you can always deliver a letter in person, talk to the office staff and hope that your application will stand out from the rest.

Set out below is sample text for an email. Don't copy it word for word!

To: Miss Jo Carter
Subject: Application to study Medicine at Haddington

Dear Miss Carter
UCAS no. 11-123456-7

As you may remember, I applied to study Medicine at Haddington University. I was disappointed to be rejected after the interview/ without an interview. I now have my A level results which are:

Chemistry A*
Biology A
History of Art A

I am writing to see if you are now able to consider me should you have any places remaining.

My head teacher supports my application and is emailing you a reference. Should you wish to contact him, his details are:
Mr C Harrow
tel: 0123 456 7891
fax: 0123 456 7892
email: c.harrow@corstorphine.sch.uk

I can be contacted at the above email address and could attend an interview at short notice.

Yours sincerely,
Gerry Hastings

Don't forget that your UCAS referee may be able to help you. Try to persuade him or her to ring the admissions officers on your behalf – he or she will find it easier to get through than you will. If your referee is unable or unwilling to ring, then he or she should, at least, email a note in support of your application. It is best if both emails arrive at the medical school at the same time. In order for your referee to be able to help you, you need to put his or her name on the UCAS application in the section that asks you to nominate someone who can act on your behalf.

If you are applying to a medical school that did not receive your UCAS application, ask your referee to email or fax a copy of the application. In general, it is best to persuade the medical school to invite you to arrange for the UCAS application to be sent.

If, despite your most strenuous efforts, you are unsuccessful, you need to consider applying again (see below). The other alternative is to use the Clearing system to obtain a place on a degree course related to medicine and hope to be accepted on the medical course after you graduate.

UCAS Adjustment process

The UCAS Adjustment option is for students who have accepted an offer of a place and then achieve higher grades. A typical case might be the student who accepts a CCC offer to study bioengineering and then achieves AAA. He or she then has a small period of time (usually a week) to register for Adjustment in order to be able to approach universities that require higher grades.

It is unlikely that potential medics would be able to gain places this way, since there are very few medical places available in the post-results period and those that are available would normally be allocated to students who applied for medicine in the first place. But if you are in this situation, there is nothing to be lost by contacting the medical schools to see if they can consider you. Details can be found on the UCAS website.

What to do if you hold an offer but miss the grades

If you have only narrowly missed the required grades, it is important that you and your referee contact the medical school to put your case before you are rejected. Sample text for another email follows below.

To: Miss Jo Carter
Subject: Application to study Medicine at Haddington

Dear Miss Carter
UCAS no. 11-123456-7

As you may know, I was holding an offer of AAA from Haddington to read Medicine. Unfortunately, I have missed the offer by one grade. My results are:

Chemistry B
Biology A
History of Art A

I am writing to see if you are still able to consider me as I am still determined to study Medicine. May I remind you that I was ill during my final examinations, and that my school contacted you about this at the time.

My head teacher supports my application and is emailing you a reference. Should you wish to contact him, his details are:
Mr C Harrow
tel: 0123 456 7891
fax: 0123 456 7892
email: c.harrow@corstorphine.sch.uk

I am prepared to retake the Chemistry exam and reapply next year if you are unable to offer me a place this year.

Yours sincerely,
Gerry Hastings

If this is unsuccessful, you need to consider retaking your A levels and applying again (see below). The other alternative is to use the Clearing system to obtain a place on a degree course related to medicine and hope to apply to a medical course after you graduate.

Retaking A levels

The grade requirements for retake candidates are normally higher than for first-timers (usually AAA). You should retake any subject where your first result was below B and you should aim for an A grade in any subject you do retake. It is often necessary to retake a B grade, especially in chemistry – take advice from the college that is preparing you for the retake.

AS and A level units can no longer be retaken in January (from January 2014). Most retake students will need to resit exams during the summer exam session. If you are retaking coursework units you will need to check when this can be done with the exam board.

Check with your college or school on their provisions for students wanting to retake. It is also possible to retake A levels at some further education colleges, although they are less likely to offer a September–January course. Interviews to discuss this are free and carry no obligation to enrol on a course, so it is worth taking the time to talk to their staff before you embark on A level retakes.

It is not possible to resit IB examinations. At this point, you would need to take an A level programme to gain an equivalent academic qualification acceptable for the course you are wishing to study. You can retake a Scottish Higher in a separate academic year and the same is true for Advanced Highers, but not in all subjects. You would have to register again for, and then resit, the Advanced Highers. The same applies for the IB examinations, as you would effectively need to start these qualifications again.

Reapplying to medical school

Many medical schools discourage retake candidates (see Table 10 on pages 152–154), so the whole business of applying again needs careful thought, hard work and a bit of luck. The choice of medical schools for your UCAS application is narrower than it was the first time round. Don't apply to the medical schools that discourage retakers unless there really are special, extenuating circumstances to explain your disappointing grades. Among the excuses that will not wash are the following.

- I wasn't feeling too good on the day of the practical exam, knocked over my Bunsen and torched the answer book.
- My dog had been ill for a week before my exams and only recovered after the last paper (and I've got a vet's certificate to prove it).

- I'd spent the month before the exams condensing my notes onto small cards so that I could revise effectively. Two days before the exams, our house was broken into and the burglar trod on my notes as he climbed through the window. The police took them away for forensic examination and didn't give them back until after the last paper (and I've got a note from the CID to prove it).

Some reasons are acceptable to even the most fanatical opponents of retake candidates:

- your own illness
- the death or serious illness of a very close relative.

Consider, in addition, your age when you took the exams. Most medical schools will accept that a candidate who was well under the age of 18 on the date of sitting A levels may deserve another attempt without being branded a 'retaker'.

These are just guidelines, and the only safe method of finding out if a medical school will accept you is to ask them. Text for a typical email is set out below. Don't follow it slavishly and do take the time to write to several medical schools before you make your final choice.

To: Miss Jo Carter
Subject: Application to study Medicine at Haddington

Dear Miss Carter
UCAS no. 11-123456-7

I hope that you will not mind my writing to you, as I know you are very busy. I am about to complete my UCAS application and I am very much hoping to apply to Haddington University to study Medicine. However, I wanted to enquire whether you would be able to consider my application as I sat my A levels last June and achieved:

Chemistry B
Biology B
Psychology C

I am retaking all three subjects this year and I expect to gain A or A* in all three. I was only just 17 years old when I sat my A levels for the first time.

I would be grateful for any feedback that you can give me.

Yours sincerely,
Gerry Hastings

Notice that the format of your email should be:

- opening paragraph
- your exam results: set out clearly and with no omissions
- any extenuating circumstances: a brief statement
- your retake plan, including the timescale
- a request for help and advice
- closing formalities.

Make sure that it is brief, clear and well presented. Apart from the care needed in making the choice of medical school, the rest of the application procedure is as described in the first section of this book.

The same advice applies if you are reapplying with qualifications other than A levels. If you did not get a place but now have the grades required, then you can reapply but make sure you talk to the medical schools first. If you have not got the grades then you need to look at what routes are available. As you cannot resit the IB, you will need to look at A levels or Foundation programmes in order to reach the requisite entry requirement for a medicine course. If you have taken Scottish Highers, depending on the subject, you are able to retake again in a new academic year. Either way, you must make sure that you gain the necessary qualifications in the next sitting – even though this will allow entry to only a handful of medical schools, you should still make contact and speak to the admissions tutors at those medical schools that consider retakes.

6 | Non-standard applications

So far, this book has been concerned with the 'standard' applicant: the UK resident who is studying at least two science subjects at A level and who is applying from school or who is retaking immediately after disappointing A levels. However, what about students who do not have this 'standard' background, such as international students? Or those who have not studied science A levels? The main non-standard applicants and the steps they should take to apply to medical school are outlined in this chapter.

Those who have not studied science A levels

If you decide that you would like to study medicine after having already started on a combination of A levels that does not fit the subject requirements for entry to medical school, you can apply for the 'pre-medical course'.

The course covers elements of chemistry, biology and physics and lasts one academic year. It leads to the first MB qualification, for which science A levels provide exemption. If your pre-med application is rejected, you will have to spend a further two years taking science A levels at a sixth-form college. Alternatively, some colleges offer one-year A level courses, and many subjects can be covered from scratch in a single year. Check which provisions your local college has to offer. However, only very able students can cover A levels in chemistry and biology in a single year with good results. You should discuss your particular circumstances with the staff of a number of colleges in order to select the course that will prepare you to achieve the A level subjects you need at the grades you require.

Overseas students

Competition for the few places available to overseas students is fierce and you would be wise to discuss your application informally with the medical school before submitting your UCAS application. Many medical schools give preference to students who do not have adequate provision for training in their own countries. You should contact the medical schools individually for advice on application procedure and costs.

Information about qualifications can be obtained from British Council offices or British embassies.

Mature students and graduates

Graduates

Course options available to graduates include the following:

- four-year graduate-entry courses
- five-/six-year courses in the normal way
- six-year pre-medical/medical courses
- Access courses.

You should check which Access courses are accepted by medical schools, as not all will consider them. Often, each medical school has a shortlist of Access courses from which it accepts applications – for example, at Keele they currently only look at Access courses from The Manchester College, College of West Anglia, Sussex Downs College and University of Sussex at Brighton. Other medical schools accept different ones. It is also usually the case that you have to reach a very high level of achievement in these courses, not just pass them.

Mature students

In recent years the options available for mature students have increased enormously. There is a growing awareness that older students often represent a 'safer' option for medical schools because they are likely to be more committed to medicine and less likely to drop out, and are able to bring to the medical world many skills and experiences that 18-year-olds sometimes lack. In general, there are two types of mature applicant:

1. those who have always wanted to study medicine but who failed to get into medical school when they applied from school in the normal way
2. those who came to the idea later on in life, often having embarked on a totally different career.

The first type of mature applicant has usually followed a degree course in a subject related to medicine and has obtained a good grade (minimum 2.i). These students have an uphill path into medicine because their early failure tends to prejudice the selectors. Nevertheless, they do not have the problem of taking science A levels at a late stage in their education. A few years ago, applicants in this position almost always had to go back to the beginning (sometimes even having to resit A levels) and then apply to the medical schools for the standard five-/six-year courses.

The second category of mature student is often of more interest to the medical school selectors and interviewers. Applications are welcomed from people who have achieved success in other careers and who can bring a breadth of experience to the medical school and to the profession.

Options available for mature students are summarised below. The chapter then examines each option in more detail.

Applicants with A levels that satisfy medical schools' standard offers

Five-/six-year courses in the normal way.

Applicants with A levels that do not satisfy standard offers

This could include arts A levels, or grades that are too low. Applicants in this category can take the following routes.

- Retake/pick up new A levels at sixth-form college.
- Enrol on a six-year pre-medical/medical course (first MBChB pre-medical entry). These are available at:
  - Bristol
  - Cardiff
  - Dundee
  - East Anglia
  - Keele
  - King's College London
  - Manchester
  - Sheffield
  - Southampton.
- These courses are usually given the code A104 by UCAS. They include a foundation (pre-medical) year and are designed for students without science A level backgrounds. They should not be confused with the six-year (usually A100) courses offered by many medical schools that include an intercalated BSc. The A100 courses require science A levels.
- Enrol on an Access course (see page 117).

Mature students with no formal A level or equivalent qualifications

Applicants in this category can take the following routes:

- A levels, then five-/six-year courses in the normal way
- Access courses (see page 117).

Preparing the application

Mature students and graduates are faced with many decisions on the route to becoming a doctor. Not only do they have to decide which course or combination of courses might be suitable, but in many cases they also have to try to gauge how best to juggle the conflicting demands of study, financial practicalities and their families.

Mature students need to prepare carefully for their applications in order to ensure that they are recognised as being fully committed to a career as a doctor. As an illustration of this, take the case of Matt Appleby.

Case study

Matt is a psychology graduate who is now studying A level Chemistry over a year. He applied to four medical schools and has offers from all of them. Matt writes:

'It is unlikely that you will encounter something as uniquely stressful and as utterly absorbing as applying to medical school.

I say this not from the perspective of a 17-year-old A level student – I already did that once and it was arduous enough – but from the position of a 27-year-old graduate. For somebody serious about applying, the process should start at least a year beforehand.

Medical schools are immensely specific in what they want from their applicants. Your application may be inappropriate for one school, but desirable to another; each medical school likes to consider itself unique in its approach. Trust me; they will impress this upon you at interviews.

The best advice I got can be summed up simply: start early. Make contact with the admissions team. I emailed asking for more and more clarification; I took any opportunity to go to meet with the admissions staff. Quite a few places, such as King's, have an open door policy, which is fantastic. So when the day comes for an interview, or even maybe a rejection, you can show your determination through a paper trail.

I now know lots of people who've applied, and for every really impressive applicant I encounter, there are at least three or four who have applied to institutions for the wrong reasons: the city it is in or friends who are there. You have to go to as many open days as possible. This is usually your only opportunity to talk to admissions tutors directly – you can tell immediately from the conversation whether you should apply there or not on the basis of what the tutor or admissions officer says. I heard it all, from some downright outrageous hostility towards graduates such as myself, to really confidence-boosting remarks about my experience.

Creating a narrative

Getting an interview is easily the hardest part of the application process, but there is a strong correlation between preparation and your chances of getting it. I found that all the things admissions tutors are looking for could easily be demonstrated in a well-crafted UCAS statement. For instance, they always want to see the capacity to deal with stressful situations. So you want to show that you have really good coping mechanisms, something like sport, running, tai chi, whatever, but make a point of saying how it helps to deal with stress. They always ask this at interviews.

Also, show how you have been in stressful situations and survived. Don't give them an account of being mugged or the death of your beloved hamster, but go out and find an experience that actually tests you. Work as a much-needed volunteer in anything from soup kitchens to nursing homes. It does not need to be medically related; it just needs to show that you are made of tough stuff. They are pretty sick of hearing "I shadowed a GP over half term"; everyone does it – I did it.

Admissions staff are always going to want to see experience, but it is all about what that experience meant to you. They seem to be far more impressed by somebody who gave an evening a week working with underprivileged children than someone who ran around behind their dad's best mate who is fortunately a top neurosurgeon. Shadowing is important to show only because it gives an insight into the workings of the NHS. Far more salient are the experiences of an applicant who performs a meaningful and thought-provoking responsibility.

The art of creating this "narrative" is in showing that you have really considered medicine carefully. You need to demonstrate the time and planning that has gone into your decision and how you have gone about accruing the necessary experiences. Without this you will be sunk in the water. That's not to say that you can't get some things together quickly. I shadowed a psychiatrist and an anaesthetist and signed up for volunteering at my local hospice all in the space of a few weeks. But these experiences are only what you make of them. Your aim is to create the story of your experience, your academic record and your capacity to bring all your great qualities to their medical school. Don't be shy. It is ruthless self-promotion.

Interviews

My biggest enemy was stress. You have been contemplating the interview for months before you even started applying, and now, in your head, it's all or nothing. For my first interview I was almost bouncing off the walls. There were so many things I wanted to say, and as the words came out of my mouth there was almost an out of body experience – like seeing yourself in the third person, trying desperately to make every point count. The only advice I can give to you about coping with the stress was what was given to me – breathe and try and keep a sense of perspective.

It is an interview, and you may think it is all or nothing, but you've got this far. It was not a fluke, you had something in your application, your experiences or your grades that made them say, "Let's hear a little more from this one."

You know it is coming, and yet, when asked, it immediately seems to bamboozle you: "So Matt, why do you want to be a doctor?"

Prepare for this question right now. Your interviewers know that you have prepared for this question, but they really do not seem to like answers that are clearly rehearsed. If you make your answer sound too practised then they will just fire questions at you until they break into something you didn't prepare for. You don't want this. I was asked what I thought the greatest stressors were on junior doctors, and I started firing off the prepared answers: MTAS [Medical Training Application Service], long hours, working nights, dealing with death on a daily basis. But they were not happy until I had run out of answers and actually was forced to sit and really think.

The interviewers are impressed with a candidate who has prepared, but they also want a doctor who can think on his feet. In all the interviews I have had they asked questions that stumped me. Let's face it, you have three or even four highly trained clinicians and practitioners interviewing you; it is right that they should be really testing. It is a cliché, but I don't care – this really is your opportunity to sell yourself. Enjoy it!

There are not always questions from medical stories in the newspapers, but I have been asked about a story that was pertinent to my personal statement. There are many medical schools that tell you in advance that you will have to consider an ethical case. For this, the best preparation is to buy a short introductory medical ethics book and take some brief notes. It is impressive when being asked an ethical question on joint replacement for you to be able to offer different perspectives. Medical ethics came up in every interview I had, and I was glad for the hours of work I'd put in. It's an interesting subject anyway.

As I was a psychology graduate, I was always being asked why I didn't want to be a psychologist. As a graduate they also always ask: "Why now?" "Why not earlier?" "What has made you change direction?" I gave an earnest answer but, in my modest opinion, keep the emotional stuff to a minimum. Interviewers do not want to hear about a life-changing event when you broke your arm or even something as sad as a death in the family. I had been working as an ambulance medic overseas and had many an emotional experience that drove me ever closer to medicine, but first and foremost I find the subject matter compelling. I am interested; I want to learn more. I want to do a job that is both financially rewarding and fulfilling. I am aware of the years of work and study and financial responsibility, and I have made a qualified and clear decision to pursue this course. This is what they want to hear.

After the interview

I remember walking out of at least two interviews and thinking the best I had done was simply okay, and I walked out of another thinking it had gone terribly. The fact is that none of these appraisals was correct. The one that had gone the worst was the institution that gave me the best offer. You just do not know what is going on in the heads of the interviewers. It is not that they are a miserable bunch of doctors, but they have a considerable responsibility and do not take it lightly. The best advice I can suggest is an insight from a professor of law I know who regularly interviews judges, postgraduates and undergraduate students. She is always nice, no matter what she thinks of the candidate. It just makes her life easier and the process more pleasant for all parties involved, but I can imagine there are many candidates who walk out thinking, "That went swimmingly, I can't believe she laughed at my joke", only to later find themselves unsuccessful.'

Matt's medical school interview questions were typical of those faced by mature students and graduates. The interviewers were interested in:

- why he had decided to change direction
- what he had done to convince himself that this was the right option for him
- what his career had given him in the way of personal qualities that were relevant to medicine
- what financial arrangements he had made to fund his studies
- whether he had found it difficult studying A levels alongside 18-year-olds.

Personal statement

Take your personal statement to as many sensible people who know what they are talking about as you can. Bribe teachers with coffee and chocolate. Go to science teachers for help, as the people reading the finished article tend to see things from a similar rationale; along the lines of 'Why is that there?' and 'What's the point of saying that? It's just waffle.' Keep the writing simple, don't overuse the thesaurus, and check spelling and punctuation to ridiculous extremes. Remember, spell check isn't foolproof and won't flag the difference between principle and principal, or effect and affect. It's the little things like that which could ruin a perfectly good application.

For mature applicants, the UCAS personal statement needs to be carefully structured. In most cases, insufficient space is allowed for the amount of information necessary to present a convincing case. It is usually advisable for mature applicants to send a detailed CV and covering letter direct to the medical schools once their UCAS number has been received.

For mature applicants, the personal statement should be structured as follows:

1. brief career and educational history: in note form or bullet points if necessary
2. reasons for the change of direction
3. what the candidate has done to investigate medicine
4. brief details of achievements, interests, etc.: again, note form or bullet points are fine.

The most important thing to bear in mind is that you must convince the selectors that you are serious about the change in direction, and that your decision to apply to study medicine is not a spur-of-the-moment reaction to dissatisfaction with your current job or studies.

A useful exercise is to try to imagine that you are the person who will read the personal statement in order to decide whether to interview or to reject without interview. Does your personal statement contain sufficient indication of thorough research, preparation and long-term commitment? If it does not, you will be rejected. As a rough guide, at least half of it should cover your reasons for applying for a medical course and the preparation and research that you have undertaken. The further back in time you can demonstrate that you started to plan your application, the stronger it will be.

Doing a pre-medical course

Pre-medical courses or programmes are not to be confused with Access courses. As the name suggests, pre-medical courses usually act as a 'pre-medical school year' or 'year zero' before you enter medical school.

You will need to look at the websites of each medical university to find out if they offer this course.

Access courses

A number of colleges of further education offer Access to Medicine courses. The best-known and most successful of these is the course at the College of West Anglia, in King's Lynn. Primarily (but not exclusively) aimed at health professionals, the course covers biology, chemistry, physics and other medically related topics, and lasts one year. Most medical schools will accept students who have successfully completed the course. Contact details can be found at the end of the book.

Four-year graduate courses

Often known as Graduate Entry Programmes (GEPs), these are given the code A101 or A102 by UCAS. These codes help you match up similar courses at different institutions and tell you which course is applicable to what you are wishing to study. The biggest change in medical school entry in recent years has been the development of these graduate-entry schemes. The first medical schools to introduce accelerated courses specifically for graduates were St George's Hospital Medical School and Leicester/Warwick (which has since split into two separate medical schools). Courses can be divided into two types:

1. those for graduates with a medically related degree
2. those that accept graduates with degrees in any discipline.

About 10% of UK medical school placements are now on GEPs. The following medical schools run GEPs (UCAS code A101/A102), further details of which can be found on the UCAS website:

- Birmingham
- Bristol
- Cambridge
- Imperial
- Keele
- King's
- Leicester
- Liverpool
- Newcastle
- Nottingham
- Oxford
- Queen Mary
- Southampton
- St George's
- Swansea
- Warwick.

The King's course differs from the others listed above, as it is also available to healthcare professionals with equivalent academic qualifications. The first year of the course is taught in London or in Kent. Students then join the other King's MBBS students for the remaining three years.

GAMSAT

Four medical schools use the GAMSAT (Graduate Australian Medical School Admissions Test). For GAMSAT enquiries, email gamsat@ucas.ac.uk or see www.gamsat.co.uk.

Standard registrations for the GAMSAT UK test take place in early June. The fee to sit the GAMSAT test is £222 but an extra charge of £60 applies if you sit the GAMSAT after 16 September. Payment must be made by credit card at the time of completing your online registration or by bank draft after completing a provisional registration. No other payment options are available.

Candidates sit the GAMSAT examination in September, and those with the best all-round scores are then called for interview. The GAMSAT examination consists of three papers:

1. reasoning in humanities and social sciences (75 multiple-choice questions) – 100 minutes
2. written communication (two essays) – 60 minutes
3. reasoning in biological and physical sciences (110 multiple-choice questions: 40% biology, 40% chemistry, 20% physics) – 170 minutes.

The medical schools that use the GAMSAT examination for their graduate courses are:

- Nottingham
- Peninsula or Exeter
- St George's
- Swansea.

Peninsula also uses the GAMSAT for anyone who has not sat A levels in the last two years. Peninsula does not offer the A101 course.

Studying outside the UK

If you are unsuccessful in gaining a place at one of the UK medical schools, and do not want to follow the graduate-entry path, you might want to look at other options. One option for those who have been unsuccessful with their applications is to study medicine abroad – for example at Charles University in the Czech Republic or Comenius University in Bratislava, the capital of Slovakia. There are a number of medical schools throughout the world that will accept A level students, but the important issue is whether or not you would be able to practise in the UK upon qualification, should you wish to do so.

Courses often attended by UK students include the following.

- St George's University School of Medicine in Grenada (West Indies) is the most popular and 'tried and tested' option, for those who can afford the fees. Students who wish to practise in the UK can spend part of the clinical stage of the course in a range of hospitals in the UK, including King's in London. To practise in the UK, students sit the PLAB (Professional and Linguistic Assessments Board) test to gain limited registration; for more information, see www.gmc-uk.org/doctors/plab.asp. Clinical experience can also be gained in hospitals in the US, allowing students to practise there as well. A high proportion of the St George's University medical school teachers have worked in UK universities and medical schools.
- There are four-year medical degree courses at St Matthew's University, Grand Cayman. The first two years are taught on Grand Cayman (British West Indies) and the final two clinical years are taught in the UK or the US.
- Six-year medical degree courses are offered in Slovakia, the Czech Republic and Poland. These courses are taught in English and are recognised in the UK.
- Medical courses are taught in English at Charles University in Prague and at other universities in the Czech Republic.

In addition to the medical schools attached to UK universities, there are a number of institutions offering medical degree courses that are taught in the UK but are accredited by overseas universities – mostly based in the Caribbean, Russia or Africa. If you are considering these, you must ensure that you are fully satisfied that the courses are bona fide and that the qualification you receive will allow you to practise in the UK (or anywhere else in the world).

In order to check if your qualification is recognised in the UK, you should visit the GMC website (www.gmc-uk.org). The GMC sets out guidelines as defined by those who are listed in the Avicenna Directory for Medicine. You can also refer to the university websites, which should inform you of the validity of their degree in the UK.

Getting into US medical schools

Here we can only point those who are interested in studying medicine in the US in the right direction. Principally, what you will need to do is go to the AAMC (Association of American Medical Colleges) website at www.aamc.org. This is an excellent site, but dense. All of the member universities are listed, and by following the links most of your questions can be answered.

Furthermore, from here you can be directed to AMCAS, which is the American Medical College Application Service. For students wishing to apply, go to www.aamc.org/students/applying. The AAMC website suggests that a very good investment is the *Medical School Admission Requirements (MSAR)* book, published in April 2012, which can be bought for around £21.

Suffice it to say here that the following criteria have to be met.

- You are expected to gain very high grades in AS/A levels – nearly all straight A grades. The higher the grades, the higher your GPA (grade point average) will be; the higher your GPA, the better your chances of being selected by the more renowned universities. An A grade = 4 GPA points; a B grade = 3; and a B+ = 3.75.
- You will be expected to sit SAT entrance tests (formerly Scholastic Aptitude Test and Scholastic Assessment Test) – these are standardised tests for college admissions in the US.
- The current SAT reasoning test is administered in about four hours and costs $50 (approximately £28) or $81 (approximately £44) for international students. There are late fees of $27.
- You will be asked to provide two or three references from your personal tutor and teachers.
- If you are not from an English-speaking country you will be required to sit the TOEFL (Test of English as a Foreign Language). The minimum score for entry into any university is 79 out of 120. The more demanding the course (such as medicine) and the more prestigious the university, the higher this language requirement will be.
- Most universities accept the IELTS (International English Language Testing System), but it must be at 7 points or above.
- Both the SAT and the TOEFL tests can be sat in the UK.
- Fees and living costs are very high. A full list can be obtained from the AAMC website.

If you are very serious about applying, you need to start as early as possible – early in the AS level year is recommended. This is because you will need to research the universities as best you can, bearing in mind that the distance does not allow for quick visits to open days as for UK universities.

In the US, medicine is a postgraduate degree. All students enter the schools after doing two years of undergraduate study. In these first two years you can study something different, but you must obviously study a science-based or pre-med course. You are also expected to gain work experience in these first two years. For more information go to www.aamc.org/students/aspiring.

Visas

If you are studying outside the EU, you will require a visa for study. The university in question will advise you on which visa you should obtain;

for example, in the USA they will advise you as to whether you require an F-1 Student or J-1 Exchange Visitor visa. You do not require a student visa for Grenada but you do require a student visa for the Cayman Islands. A good place to look first would be UKCISA (UK Council for International Student Affairs) at www.ukcisa.org.uk.

Students with disabilities and special educational needs

If a candidate has a specific health requirement or disability there is every possibility that a medical school will be able to help. There is an area in the personal details section of the UCAS application where you can indicate the type of disability/special needs that you have. You need to select the most appropriate option from the list given. There is also a space provided for you to give any further details of the conditions that affect you.

However, each medical school has a responsibility to ensure that doctors are able to fulfil their responsibilities. The decision on fitness to practise is separate from the academic and non-academic selection process. These guidelines are set out by the GMC. You are encouraged to fully research the demands of the course before you apply at each institution. Bear in mind that in order to practise as a doctor you also have to be deemed fit to practise. The profession places huge demands on the individual and therefore you must consider all the facts from the outset.

You are equally encouraged to apply if you have a hearing or visual impairment. All institutions are fully committed to support students with special needs, from dyslexia to physical disability, and have access arrangements in place.

Once an offer is made, the medical school will contact you to discuss any appropriate arrangements that should be made. It is most likely to be the case that certain halls of residence may have physical limitations on access arrangements. It is absolutely vital that all relevant information that may impair your ability to study and potentially practise is made clear at this stage. If not, and if the issues become obvious later on in the course, it could possibly result in the candidate being withdrawn from the course.

In terms of special educational needs, students who require a word processor or extra time will be allowed these in the same way that they would have been at school, subject to providing the correct documentation to the university.

For more information refer directly to the university.

Some useful websites

Access-Ability: www.access-ability.org
Hope for Disabled Doctors: www.hope4medics.co.uk
Assist UK: www.assist-uk.org

7 | Fees and funding

As you are probably aware, there have been significant changes to the fees and funding structure for universities, which came into effect in the 2012 academic year. These changes are due to the Coalition Government removing the subsidised funding for university courses, and therefore raising the cap on the fees universities are allowed to charge students.

To find out the fees and funding for medical courses, prospective students should explore each of the universities' websites and/or talk to the universities' financial departments. This is because fees and funding procedures vary from university to university. Factors affecting the fees and overall debt can include:

- where the student is from
- geographic (does the student live in a city?)
- the amount of help that parents can give
- if the student receives a scholarship
- whether the student has found work.

Whatever the circumstances, a student must give serious consideration to the cost and be prepared to fully commit. Your choice also has to involve careful financial planning for the four or five years that a course may last. On top of the tuition fees, you will have to consider living costs; needless to say, in big cities such as London, living costs will be much higher than in other parts of the country. One estimate is that London will cost about £10,555 per year to cover food, accommodation, travel and books.

Fees

UK students

The government adjustments from 2012 entry in respect of university tuition fees have meant the following changes for UK students.

Universities are now allowed to charge UK and EU students up to £9,000 a year for tuition fees. Most of the higher ranked universities will charge the maximum amount. The average course fee across all institutions will be £8,500. You should refer to the websites of the specific universities to find out what they intend to charge, and also to the UCAS website, using the 'Course Search' facility.

If you are a student resident in England you could pay up to £9,000 wherever you study in the UK. If you are a student resident in Scotland you will not pay any tuition fees if you study at a Scottish university. You will pay up to £9,000 if you study elsewhere in the UK. If you are a student resident in Wales you will pay up to £9,000 wherever you study in the UK. However, you will be able to receive a £3,465 loan from the Welsh Government, and you will also be eligible for a grant of up to £5,535. If you are a student resident in Northern Ireland you will pay up to £9,000 if you study in England, Wales or Scotland, but you will pay only £3,465 if you study in Northern Ireland. Students from Northern Ireland will be able to apply for a tuition fee loan of up to £9,000 per annum.

EU students

If you are an EU student you will pay up to £9,000 if you study in England or Northern Ireland, but there is no fee if you study in Scotland. You will receive the same help as Welsh students (see above) if you are studying at a Welsh university.

International students

Home students – that is, UK nationals – and EU students pay lower tuition fees than non-EU/UK students. For international students from outside these two regions, the costs can be prohibitive. The fees for non-EU international students do not have a set upper limit – they will depend on the course and the university. For example, King's College London will charge students £17,800 for years 1 and 2 and £33,000 for years 3 to 5.

In the past two academic years the tuition fees charged to these students were typically between £14,000 and £19,000 per year for the pre-clinical courses and between £21,000 and £39,000 per year for the clinical courses.

This can be even higher; for example for 2012 entry, Imperial College charged £27,500 per year for international students in years 1 to 3 and then £39,150 for years 4 to 6. This amounts to £199,950 in total, consistent since 2007.

Nevertheless, whether you are a UK/EU resident or an international student, the truth of the matter is that, unless you are wealthy, the usual scenario is that you will accumulate a large debt.

Funding: bursaries and grants

Universities charging more than £6,000 must provide financial support for students from disadvantaged backgrounds. You can find out about this at:

- www.ucas.com/students/studentfinance, or
- www.gov.uk/browse/education/student-finance.

In England, you can apply for a maintenance grant to cover your living costs. This is based on your overall household income. The maximum you can receive is £3,354 if your household income is less than £25,000. In Scotland there are different types of grants available for dependants (£2,640) or lone parents (£1,305).

Changes to funding

According to Money4Medstudents (www.money4medstudents.org), the following changes have been made to funding.

- Students will not pay tuition fees before they start or while they are studying a course.
- You may apply for a student loan, which is not income-assessed.
- In the fifth and later years of your course, loans will be paid in full by the NHS Student Grants Unit.
- Starting from 2009–10, if household income is £25,000 or less, students have been eligible to receive the full maintenance grant.
- Starting from 2009–10, students with a household income of over £50,020 are not entitled to a maintenance grant.
- There have been increases in the Disabled Students' Allowance.
- There have been major changes to income assessment for new and continuing students from Scotland.

NHS bursary

Students studying medicine are eligible for a means-tested NHS bursary to help with any day-to-day living costs. These bursaries will be available for medical students, as medical degrees are recognised as an NHS-funded course. The bursary usually covers the course fees and other practical costs. All new and prospective students are eligible to apply and students who are awarded these bursaries can also apply for student loans.

NHS bursaries are available for full- and part-time students. To be eligible for such a bursary a student must qualify as a home student and be on a course that is accepted as an NHS-funded place. For more information, the NHS student website at www.nhsbsa.nhs.uk/Students is useful.

Applications checklist (according to NHS Business Services Authority)

- Regardless of nationality, you must be considered to be ordinarily living in the UK and/or a UK country, as well as being settled in the UK under the Immigration Act 1971.

- In order to apply for the bursary, you must be given a conditional or unconditional offer at any university or higher education institution in England (other countries will apply the same conditions to their specific universities).
- Once received, the university or higher education institution will pass your details on to NHS Student Bursaries who will then contact you with your student reference number and details of where you can obtain the relevant application form on their website.
- From the academic year 2009–10 onwards, all students applying for a bursary are required to submit original documentation with their forms, i.e. a driver's licence or a passport.
- Applications should be submitted as soon as possible. The NHS bursary application form should be submitted within nine months of the first day of the course. For example, if your first day is 1 September 2014, then the last date that you can submit the application form is 31 May 2015.

It is also worth finding out from universities if scholarships are available. According to the NHS website, in the 2011–12 academic year, the Department of Health agreed to pay the tuition fee contribution for each student affected, up to a maximum amount of £3,375. These funding arrangements will be the same for the 2013–14 and 2014–15 academic years. This amount cannot be exceeded under any circumstances, and therefore if a university charges higher fees than this amount in the academic year, students will be expected to meet the balance them-selves.

National Scholarship Programme (NSP) (for students resident in England)

Any students whose family's income is less than £25,000 per year will be eligible for help from the NSP. This can take the form of help with tuition fees, accommodation or other costs. The university will pay the scholarship and so the nature and size of the scholarship will vary from institution to institution. You can find out more about this at www.gov.uk/government/uploads/system/uploads/attachment_data/file/32417/11-730-national-scholarship-programme-year-one.pdf.

Student loans

The most common way in which students are able to fund themselves is by taking out a student loan, of which there are two types: a loan for fees and a loan for living costs. Students start repaying these loans only once they have finished studying and are earning over £21,000. Most universities can put you in touch with loan agencies and with the NHS.

How to apply for financial support: UK students

New students in England

- Ask for an application form from the local authority (LA) in whose area you normally live.
- Ask for an application form from the Student Loan Company (SLC) if you live in an area testing the new finance arrangements.
- Apply online or download a form (form PN1) from the Student Finance England website (www.sfengland.slc.co.uk).

New students in Northern Ireland

- Ask for an application form from the Education and Library Board (ELB) in whose area you normally live.
- Apply online or download a form (form PN1) from the Student Finance Northern Ireland website (www.studentfinanceni.co.uk).

New students in Wales

- Apply to the LA in whose area you normally live.
- Apply online or download a form (form PN1) from the Student Finance Wales website (www.studentfinancewales.co.uk).

New students in Scotland

- Apply to the Student Awards Agency for Scotland (SAAS) wherever you live in Scotland.
- Apply online or download a form (form SAS3) from the SAAS website (www.saas.gov.uk).

Other sources of funding for medical students

There are various websites that will give you information on a variety of organisations that can offer scholarships, grants and bursaries that are in addition to the NHS bursary. These include the following.

- **Access Agreement bursaries:** non-repayable bursaries, typically of £310 upwards, for students receiving the full maintenance grant or special support grant (except in Scotland, where a fee waiver or bursary scheme may be an alternative for students from Scotland).
- **Armed forces bursaries/cadetships:** these are generous and may be worth considering, provided you are happy to commit to an agreed number of years working as a doctor in the Army, Navy or Air Force.

- **Medical awards and competitions:** these are of varying amounts and varying levels of competitiveness.
- **University bursaries:** many universities often provide bursaries for low-income students. If your household income is below £17,910 you will probably receive a bursary of at least £305. However, some bursaries are more than this and some universities give bursaries to people with higher incomes. It is worth investigating this with your university.
- **Hardship loans:** if you are having financial problems you can apply for additional sources of funding; up to £500 can be added to your current student loan.

For more information on these, go to www.medschoolsonline.co.uk.

Scholarships and prizes

There are also many scholarships and prizes that are run by the many professional medical organisations. Some of the applications may require a supporting statement from a member of academic staff. Check the criteria carefully before applying.

- **British Association of Dermatologists:** offers £5,000 towards fees and living expenses for an intercalated-year project related to dermatology and skin biology. It also offers £500 as undergraduate project grants.
- **Sir John Ellis Student Prizes:** students submit a description of a piece of work, survey, research or innovation in which they have been directly involved in the field of medical education. First prize in each category is £300 plus expenses (conference fee, accommodation in halls of residence, annual dinner and standard travel expenses). Runners-up will have the conference fee and accommodation in the halls of residence paid for.
- **The Genetics Society Summer Studentship scheme:** this provides funding for undergraduate students to spend their summer vacation working in a genetics laboratory in order to gain research experience. There are grants available of up to £3,000.
- **The Nuffield Foundation:** a scheme similar to the Genetics Society Summer Studentship is also run by the Nuffield Foundation.
- **The Physiological Society:** the Society offers grants of up to £150 per week for students undertaking research of a physiologic nature under the supervision of a member of the society during a summer vacation or intercalated BSc year (if the student is not receiving LA or other government support).
- **The Pathological Society:** funding is offered for students wanting to intercalate a BSc in pathology who do not have LA or other government support. The Society also offers awards to fund electives and vacation studies in pathology.

Fees for studying abroad

You should not expect the same level of financial support if you want to study overseas. You do have the right as a UK citizen to study in Europe and you can find out more about financial support on the Your Europe website at www.europa.eu/youreurope/citizens. There are a few grants and scholarships available through UK charities, and these are listed on the UKCISA (www.ukcisa.org.uk) and UNESCO (www.unesco.org.uk) websites.

8 | Careers in medicine

This chapter looks briefly at some of the possible routes open to prospective medics. It is of value to have an idea and indeed some understanding of the possibilities and avenues open to you both while you are studying and for the interview. Arguably some knowledge here could be of great benefit if you are asked questions such as 'Have you given any thought to future prospects?' or 'Where do you see yourself in 10 years?' at interview.

The paths and avenues open to members of the medical profession once they graduate are too numerous to go into in detail here. As a trainee doctor nearing the end of your study, questions such as the prospect and possibility of specialisation and about where you might like to work have to be answered. The best advice I can give here is to make sure to research as much as possible, talk to people and, above all, be aware of the areas in medicine that you have enjoyed the most.

Apart from specialisations (see below), there is a wide range of areas that doctors may end up working in. Obviously, most people understand that many doctors become GPs. However, there are also as many who dedicate their lives to working in the state-funded NHS. Within the NHS there is a panoply of possibilities, such as working in public health, working in medical management and administration and even working in research.

Away from public hospitals, there are careers to be made in private enterprise, for example running a consultancy business such as plastic surgery. Some doctors opt for the armed forces and others work for the police as forensic psychiatrists and forensic pathologists. Another area is education, in terms of lecturing, research and writing while working for a university. It is not uncommon to find doctors who have a portfolio of work, spending some of their time in hospitals, doing private consultancy in their own surgeries and teaching or doing research. Such a life is not only well remunerated but also stimulating.

First job

The training programme for doctors called Modernising Medical Careers (MMC) became fully functional in 2007. The training is part of the Certificate of Completion of Training (CCT). Before the MMC, newly qualified doctors would spend a year at Pre-registration House Officer level, dividing the period between medicine and surgery. After that, the junior doctor would be working as a Senior House Officer (SHO) for a number of years before applying for a Specialist Registrar post.

MMC is summarised in Figure 6.

In the last year of the medical degree, medical students apply for a place on the Foundation programme. The Foundation programme is designed to provide structured postgraduate training on the job and lasts two years. The job starts a few weeks after graduating from medical school. In the first few weeks there might be a short period of 'shadowing', to help new doctors get used to the job. After successful completion of the first year, they will gain registration with the GMC.

The Foundation programme job is divided into three four-month posts in the first year. These posts will typically consist of:

- four months of surgery (e.g. urology, general surgery)
- four months of another specialty (e.g. psychiatry, GP)
- four months in a medical specialty (e.g. respiratory, geriatrics).

The second year is again divided into three four-month posts, but here the focus is perhaps on a specialty or may include other jobs in shortage areas.

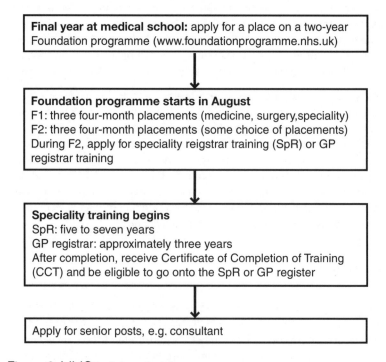

Figure 6 MMC training structure

For more information on the application procedure, visit:

- www.medschoolsonline.co.uk/index.php?pageid=157
- www.foundationprogramme.nhs.uk
- www.mmc.nhs.uk.

Specialisations

The MMC was introduced in 2007. It aims to provide information to doctors applying for specialty training within the NHS in England. It provides details on how to apply and the changes that occur to the recruitment and the application process. 2012 is the first year in which an agreed standardised timetable has been produced for all applicants by all of the UK health departments.

Specialist training programmes typically last for five to seven years. After gaining the CCT, a doctor is then eligible to apply for a Certificate of Eligibility for Specialist Registration (CESR). Either will make you eligible for entry to the GMC's Specialist Register or GP Register.

To do this you will need to apply for postgraduate medical training programmes in the UK with the deanery or 'unit of application' directly. In this application process you will be competing for places on specialty training programmes with other doctors at similar levels of competence and experience.

For more information, visit the MMC website at www.mmc.nhs.uk.

Here follow the 10 major specialisations available in medicine, each with its own sub-specialisations and some selected elaborations:

1. accident and emergency
2. anaesthetics
3. general practice
4. intensive care
5. medical specialties
   - cardiovascular disease
   - clinical genetics
   - clinical pharmacology and therapeutics
   - dermatology
   - endocrinology and diabetes mellitus
   - gastroenterology
   - general medicine
   - genito-urinary medicine
   - geriatrics
   - infectious diseases
   - medical oncology
   - nephrology (renal medicine)

- o neurology
- o occupational medicine
- o paediatrics
- o palliative medicine
- o rehabilitation medicine
- o rheumatology
- o tropical medicine
6. obstetrics and gynaecology
7. pathology
    - o bacteriology
    - o blood transfusion
    - o chemical pathology
    - o diagnostic radiology
    - o forensic pathology
    - o haematology
    - o histopathology
    - o immunology
    - o medical microbiology
    - o neuropathology
    - o radiology
    - o radiology and nuclear medicine
    - o radiotherapy
8. psychiatry
    - o adult psychiatry
    - o child and adolescent psychiatry
    - o forensic psychiatry
    - o old age psychiatry
    - o psychiatry of learning difficulties
9. public health medicine
    - o clinical public health
    - o government medical service
    - o medical administration
10. surgical specialties
    - o general surgery
    - o neurosurgery
    - o ophthalmology
    - o otolaryngology
    - o paediatric surgery
    - o plastic surgery
    - o thoracic surgery
    - o urology.

Below are a few selected specialisations, which are briefly described.

Anaesthetist

An anaesthetist is a medical doctor trained to administer anaesthesia and manage the medical care of patients before, during and after surgery. Anaesthetists are the single largest group of hospital doctors and their skills are used throughout the hospital in patient care. They have a medical background to deal with many emergency situations.

They are also trained to deal with breathing, resuscitation of the heart and lungs and advanced life support.

Audiologist

Audiologists identify and assess hearing and/or balance disorders, and from this will recommend and provide appropriate rehabilitation for the patient. The main areas of work are paediatrics, adult assessment and rehabilitation, special needs groups and research and development.

Cardiologist

This is the branch of medicine that deals with disorders of the heart and blood vessels. These specialists deal with the diagnosis and treatment of heart defects, heart failure and valvular heart disease.

Dermatologist

There are over 2,000 recognised diseases of the skin but about 20 of these account for 90% of the workload. Dermatologists are specialist physicians who diagnose and treat diseases of the skin, hair and nails such as severe acne in teenagers, which happens to be a very common reason for referral. Inflammatory skin diseases such as eczema and psoriasis are very common and without treatment can produce significant disability.

Gastroenterologist

A gastroenterologist is a medically qualified specialist who has sub-specialised in the diseases of the digestive system, which include ailments affecting all organs, from mouth to anus, along the alimentary canal. In all, a gastroenterologist undergoes a minimum of 13 years of formal classroom education and practical training before becoming a certified gastroenterologist.

General practitioner (GP)

A GP is a medical practitioner who specialises in family medicine and primary care. They are often referred to as family doctors and work in consultation clinics based in the local community.

GPs can work on their own or in a group practice with other doctors and healthcare providers. A GP treats acute and chronic illnesses and provides care and health education for all ages. They are called GPs because they look after a whole person, and this includes their mental health and physical well-being.

Gynaecologist

Gynaecologists have a broad base of knowledge and can vary their professional focus on different disorders and diseases of the female reproductive system. This includes preventive care, prenatal care and detection of sexually transmitted diseases, smear test screening and family planning. They may choose to specialise in different areas, such as acute and chronic medical conditions, for example cervical cancer, infertility, urinary tract disorders and pregnancy and delivery.

Immunologist

Immunologists are responsible for investigating the functions of the body's immune system. They help to treat diseases such as AIDS/HIV, allergies (e.g. asthma, hay fever) and leukaemia using complex and sophisticated molecular techniques. They deal with the understanding of the processes and effects of inappropriate stimulation that are associated with allergies and transplant rejection, and may be heavily involved with research. An immunologist works within clinical and academic settings as well as with industrial research. Their role involves measuring components of the immune system, including cells, antibodies and other proteins. They develop new therapies, which involve looking at how to improve methods for treating different conditions.

Neurologist

A neurologist is a medical doctor who has trained in the diagnosis and treatment of nervous system disorders, which includes diseases of the brain, spinal cord, nerves and muscles. Neurologists perform medical examinations of the nerves of the head and neck, muscle strength and movement, balance, ambulation and reflexes, memory, speech, language and other cognitive abilities.

Obstetrician

These are specialised doctors who deal with problems that arise during maternity care, treating any complications that develop in pregnancy and childbirth and any that arise after the birth. Some obstetricians may specialise in a particular aspect of maternity care such as maternal medicine, which involves looking after the mother's health; labour care, which involves care during the birth; and/or foetal medicine, which involves looking after the health of the unborn baby.

Paediatrician

This is a physician who deals with the growth, development and health of children from birth to adolescence. To become paediatricians, doctors must complete six years of extra training after they finish their medical training. There are general paediatricians and specialist paediatricians such as paediatric cardiologists. They work in private practices or hospitals.

Plastic surgeon

Plastic surgery is the medical and cosmetic specialty that involves the correction of form and function. There are two main types of plastic surgery: cosmetic and reconstructive.

1. Cosmetic surgery procedures alter a part of the body that the person is not satisfied with, such as breast implants or fat removal.
2. Reconstructive plastic surgery involves correcting physical birth defects, such as cleft palates, or defects that occur as a result of disease treatments, such as breast reconstruction after a mastectomy, or from accidents, such as third-degree burns after a fire.

Plastic surgery includes a variety of fields such as hand surgery, burn surgery, microsurgery and paediatric surgery.

Psychiatrist

Psychiatrists are trained in the medical, psychological and social components of mental, emotional and behavioural disorders. They specialise in the prevention, diagnosis and treatment of mental, addictive and emotional disorders such as anxiety, depression, psychosis, substance abuse and developmental disabilities. They prescribe medications, practise psychotherapy and help patients and their families cope with stress and crises. Psychiatrists often consult with primary care physicians, psychotherapists, psychologists and social workers.

Surgeon

A general surgeon is a physician who has been educated and trained in diagnosis, operative and post-operative treatment, and management of patient care. Surgery requires extensive knowledge of anatomy, emergency and intensive care, nutrition, pathology, shock and resuscitation, and wound healing. Surgeons may practise in specific fields such as general surgery, orthopaedic, neurological or vascular and many more.

Urologist

A urologist is a physician who has specialised knowledge and skills regarding problems of the male and female urinary tract and the male reproductive organs. Extensive knowledge of internal medicine, paediatrics, gynaecology and other specialties is required by the urologist.

Some alternative careers

Armed forces

Doctors in the army are also officers, and provide medical care for soldiers and their families (www.gov.uk/government/organisations/ministry-of-defence/about/recruitment).

Aviation medicine (also aerospace medicine)

The main role is to assess the fitness to fly of pilots, cabin crew and infirm passengers (www.fom.ac.uk).

Clinical forensic medical examiner (police surgeon)

Clinical forensic physicians or medical examiners spend much of their time examining people who have been arrested. Detainees either ask to see a doctor or need to be examined to see if they are fit for interview or fit to be detained (www.forensic-science-society.org.uk).

Coroner

The coroner is responsible for inquiring into violent, sudden and unexpected, unnatural or suspicious deaths. Few are doctors, but some have qualifications in both medicine and law (see the section on clinical forensic and legal medicine on the Royal Society of Medicine website at www.rsm.ac.uk).

Pharmaceutical medicine

Job opportunities for doctors in pharmaceutical medicine include clinical research, medical advisory positions and becoming the medical director of a company. Patient contact is limited but still possible in the clinical trials area (www.abpi.org.uk).

Prison medicine

A prison medical officer provides healthcare, usually in the form of GP clinics, to prison inmates (www.cblocums.com/hm_prisons).

Public health practitioner

Public health medicine is a specialty that deals with health at the level of a general population rather than at the level of the individual. The role can vary from responding to outbreaks of disease that need a rapid response, such as food poisoning, to the long-term planning of health-care (www.fph.org.uk).

9 | Further information

Courses

Future Doctors

Students often have a variety of reasons for wanting to dedicate their professional lives to medicine. However, each aspiring 'future doctor' must ensure that this career choice has been an informed one. In essence, panels look for each applicant to be able to map out the next 14 years of their lives, identifying what skills they would need to develop at each step of the career ladder in order to achieve their goal of expertise in a specialty of their choice. The slow and steady progression provides a career that is often both physically and mentally demanding yet fulfilling, as the doctors' input into the multidisciplinary team results in better patient care.

It is impossible to get a true idea of what medicine entails from just attending a course or talking to careers advisers. However, there are some organisations that aim to help students gain a realistic impression of medicine as a whole. Future Doctors is one such organisation.

Future Doctors specialises in helping students in their preparation for the highly competitive medical school application process through guidance on interview skills, UKCAT and BMAT. It hosts weekend courses at Imperial and UCL, organises work experience/mentoring programmes and has an online resource dedicated to getting you into medical school. For more information contact Dr Michael Zemenides at www.futuredoctors.co.uk.

Future Doctors hosts a variety of weekend events at medical schools in London for students over the age of 15 and further details of these are given below. The organisation also works alongside charitable careers guidance companies around the UK, sending doctors into schools to give 'insight into medicine' seminars. It has a mailing list on its website and by subscribing to this you will be kept up to date with all of its events and receive a monthly medical bulletin.

The Future Doctors events include a two-day Commitment to Medicine Certificate course designed to give each student exposure to both preclinical and clinical aspects of the medical curriculum taught in medical schools around the UK. NHS doctors cover the cardiovascular, respiratory and digestive systems in detail, with an in-depth guide to the personal statement, interview, and UKCAT and BMAT aspects of the medical school application process. On the second day, specialists give talks on six different sub-specialties, going through common clinical scenarios they face on a day-to-day basis and how the multidisciplinary team goes about the investigation and treatment of each case.

There is a Clinical Skills Certificate course that allows students to be tutored in a small group setting by doctors over a weekend. This course is divided into a theory-based 'making a diagnosis day' where students are taken step by step through each stage of the diagnostic pathway. The second day is purely hands-on: students learn basic surgical skills, examination techniques and practical procedures.

There is also an online course that you can take if you cannot make any of these events.

If you are interested in finding out more, please visit www.futuredoctors. co.uk.

Publications

Careers in medicine

A Career in Medicine: Do You Have What it Takes? (2nd edition), ed. Rameen Shakur, Royal Society of Medicine Press

Careers Uncovered: Medicine, Paul Greer, Trotman

The Insider's Guide to UK Medical Schools, eds Sally Girgis, Leigh Bisset, David Burke, BMJ Books

Learning Medicine: How to Become and Remain a Good Doctor, Peter Richards, Simon Stockill, Rosalind Foster, Elizabeth Ingall, Cambridge University Press

Genetics

The Blind Watchmaker, Richard Dawkins, Penguin

Genome, Matt Ridley, Fourth Estate

The Language of the Genes, Steve Jones, Flamingo

Who's Afraid of Human Cloning? Gregory E. Pence, Rowman and Littlefield

Y: The Descent of Man, Steve Jones, Abacus

Higher education entry

HEAP 2014: University Degree Course Offers, Trotman

Getting into Oxford & Cambridge: 2014 entry, Trotman

How to Complete Your UCAS Application: 2014 entry, Trotman

Preparing for the BMAT, Heinemann

The UCAS Guide to Getting into University and College, UCAS

Medical science: general

Asimov's New Guide to Science, Isaac Asimov, Penguin

Aspirin: The Extraordinary Story of a Wonder Drug, Diarmuid Jeffreys, Bloomsbury

Don't Die Young, Dr Alice Roberts, Bloomsbury

Everything You Need to Know About Bird Flu and What You Can Do to Prepare For It, Jo Revill, Rodale

The Greatest Benefit to Mankind: A Medical History of Humanity, Roy Porter, Fontana

The Human Brain: A Guided Tour, Susan Greenfield, Phoenix

Human Instinct, Robert Winston, Bantam

The Noonday Demon: An Anatomy of Depression, Andrew Solomon, Vintage

Pain: The Science of Suffering (Maps of the Mind), Patrick Wall, Weidenfeld and Nicolson

Penicillin Man: Alexander Fleming and the Antibiotic Revolution, Kevin Brown, History Press

From Poison Arrows to Prozac: How Deadly Toxins Changed Our Lives Forever, Stanley Feldman, John Blake Publishing

A Short History of Nearly Everything, Bill Bryson, Black Swan

A User's Guide to the Brain, John Ratey, Abacus

Medical ethics

The Body Hunters: Testing New Drugs on the World's Poorest Patients, Sonia Shah, The New Press

Causing Death and Saving Lives: The Moral Problems of Abortion, Infanticide, Suicide, Euthanasia, Capital Punishment, War and Other Life-or-death Choices, Jonathan Glover, Penguin

Medical practice

Bedside Stories: Confessions of a Junior Doctor, Michael Foxton, Atlantic Books

NHS Plc: The Privatisation of Our Health Care, Allyson M. Pollock, Verso

Websites

All the medical schools have their own websites (see below) and there are numerous useful and interesting medical sites. These can be found using search engines. Particularly informative sites include the following.

- Admissions forum: www.newmediamedicine.com (essential information for applicants)
- BMAT: www.bmat.org.uk
- BMA: www.bma.org.uk
- Department of Health: www.dh.gov.uk
- GMC: www.gmc-uk.org
- Student BMJ: student.bmj.com
- UKCAT: www.ukcat.ac.uk
- UKMS: www.ukmedicalschools.com
- WHO: www.who.int

Financial advice

For information on the financial side of five to six years at medical school, see www.money4medstudents.org. This website has been prepared by the Royal Medical Benevolent Fund, in partnership with the BMA Medical Students Committee, the Council of Heads of Medical Schools and the National Association of Student Money Advisers.

Examiners' reports

The examining boards provide detailed reports on recent exam papers, including mark schemes and specimen answers. Schools are sent these every year by the boards. They are useful when analysing your performance in tests and mock examinations. If your school does not have copies, they can be obtained from the boards themselves. The examining boards' website addresses are:

- www.aqa.org.uk
- www.edexcel.com
- www.ocr.org.uk
- www.wjec.co.uk

Contact details

Studying in the UK

Aberdeen
School of Medicine and Dentistry
University of Aberdeen
3rd Floor Polwarth Building
Foresterhill
Aberdeen AB25 2ZD
Tel: 01224 437923
Email: medadm@abdn.ac.uk
Web: www.abdn.ac.uk/medicine-dentistry

Barts and The London
School of Medicine and Dentistry
Garrod Building
Turner Street
London E1 2AD
Tel: 020 7882 8478
Email: smdadmissions@qmul.ac.uk
Web: www.smd.qmul.ac.uk

Birmingham
College of Medical and Dental Sciences
University of Birmingham
Edgbaston
Birmingham B15 2TT
Tel: 0121 414 3858
Email: mdsenquiries@contacts.bham.ac.uk
Web: www.medicine.bham.ac.uk

Brighton and Sussex Medical School
BSMS Teaching Building
University of Sussex
Brighton BN1 9PX
Tel: 01273 643528
Email: medadmissions@bsms.ac.uk
Web: www.bsms.ac.uk

Bristol
Medical School
University of Bristol
Senate House
Tyndall Avenue
Bristol BS8 1TH
Tel: 0117 928 7679
Email: med-admissions@bristol.ac.uk
Web: www.bris.ac.uk/medical-school

Cambridge
University of Cambridge
School of Clinical Medicine
Addenbrookes Hospital
Hills Road
Cambridge CB2 0SP
Tel: 01223 333308
Email: admissions@cam.ac.uk
Web: www.medschl.cam.ac.uk

Cardiff
Cardiff University School of Medicine
Cochrane Medical Education Centre
Heath Park
Cardiff CF14 4YU
Tel: 029 20 68 8113
Email: medadmissions@cardiff.ac.uk
Web: www.medicine.cf.ac.uk

Dundee
Admissions and Student Recruitment
University of Dundee
2 Airlie Place
Dundee DD1 4HQ
Tel: 01382 383838
Email: contactus@dundee.ac.uk
Web: www.medicine.dundee.ac.uk

Durham
Durham University
School of Medicine, Pharmacy and Health
Wolfson Research Institute
Queen's Campus
Stockton on Tees TS17 6BH
Tel: 0191 3340353
Email: medicine.admissions@durham.ac.uk
Web: www.dur.ac.uk/school.health
Note: Durham is exactly the same as Newcastle, which sets Durham's criteria and receives all the applications, although interviews do take place at Durham.

East Anglia
Medical Admissions
Norwich Medical School
University of East Anglia
Norwich Research Park
Norwich NR4 7TJ
Tel: 01603 591515
Email: med.ug.admiss@uea.ac.uk
Web: www.uea.ac.uk/med

Edinburgh
College of Medicine and Veterinary Medicine
University of Edinburgh
The Chancellor's Building, 2nd Floor
49 Little France Crescent
Edinburgh EH16 4SB
Tel: 0131 242 6407
Email: medug@ed.ac.uk
Web: www.ed.ac.uk/schools-departments/medicine-vet-medicine

Glasgow
University of Glasgow
School of Medicine
Wolfson Medical School Building
University Avenue
Glasgow G12 8QQ
Tel: 0141 330 6216
Email: med-sch-admissions@glasgow.ac.uk
Web: www.gla.ac.uk/colleges/mvls

Hull York
Hull York Medical School
John Hughlings Jackson Building
University of York
Heslington
York YO10 5DD
Tel: 01904 321762
Email: admissions@hyms.ac.uk
Web: www.hyms.ac.uk

Imperial College
Imperial College London
South Kensington Campus
London SW7 2AZ
Tel: 020 7594 7259
Email: medicine.ug.admissions@imperial.ac.uk
Web: www.ic.ac.uk/medicine

Keele
School of Medicine
David Weatherall Building
Keele University
Staffordshire ST5 5BG
Tel: 01782 733937
Email: medicine@keele.ac.uk
Web: www.keele.ac.uk/health/schoolofmedicine

King's College London
School of Medicine
King's College London
Hodgkin Building
Guy's Campus
London SE1 1UL
Tel: 020 7848 6501
Email: ug-healthadmissions@kcl.ac.uk
Web: www.kcl.ac.uk/medicine

Leeds
Faculty of Medicine and Health
Room 10.110
Worsley Building
University of Leeds
Leeds LS2 9JT
Tel: 0113 343 4362
Email: ugmadmissions@leeds.ac.uk
Web: www.leeds.ac.uk/medhealth

Leicester
University of Leicester
Medical School
Maurice Shock Building
PO Box 138
University Road
Leicester LE1 9HN
Tel: 0116 252 2969/2985
Email: med-admis@le.ac.uk
Web: www2.le.ac.uk/departments/msce/undergraduate/medicine

Liverpool
School of Medicine
University of Liverpool
Cedar House
Ashton Street
Liverpool L69 3GE
Tel: 0151 795 4362
Web: www.liv.ac.uk/sme
Note: Lancaster University has an affiliated programme with Liverpool. Candidates need to use L41 institution code (Liverpool) but A105 as a course code. The entry criteria will be the same, and the point of contact will be Dr Karen Grant at Lancaster University.

Manchester
The Medical School
Faculty of Medical and Human Sciences
University of Manchester
Oxford Road
Manchester M13 9PL
Tel: 0161 306 0460
Email: medicine.enquiries@manchester.ac.uk
Web: www.medicine.manchester.ac.uk

Newcastle
The Medical School
University of Newcastle
Framlington Place
Newcastle upon Tyne NE2 4HH
Tel: 0191 222 7005
Web: www.ncl.ac.uk/biomedicine

Nottingham
Medical School
Faculty of Medicine and Health Sciences
University of Nottingham
Queen's Medical Centre
Nottingham NG7 2UH
Tel: 0115 823 0000
Email: medschool@nottingham.ac.uk
Web: www.nottingham.ac.uk/mhs

Oxford
Medical Sciences Teaching Centre
South Parks Road
Oxford OX1 3PL
Tel: 01865 228975
Email: lesley.maitland@medsci.ox.ac.uk
Web: www.medsci.ox.ac.uk

Peninsula Medical School
Peninsula College of Medicine and Dentistry
John Bull Building
Plymouth PL6 8BU
Tel: 01752 437444
Email: info@pcmd.ac.uk
Web: www.pcmd.ac.uk

Queen's Belfast
School of Medicine, Dentistry and Biomedical Sciences
Health Sciences Building
97 Lisburn Road
Belfast BT9 7BL

Tel: 02890 973838
Email: pjmedschool@qub.ac.uk
Web: www.qub.ac.uk/cm

St Andrews

School of Medicine
University of St Andrews
Medical and Biological Sciences Building
North Haugh
St Andrews KY16 9TF
Tel: 01334 463599
Email: admissions@st-andrews.ac.uk; medicine@st-and.ac.uk
Web: medicine.st-andrews.ac.uk

St George's

University of London
Cranmer Terrace
London SW17 0RE
Tel: 020 8725 2333
Email: enquiries@sgul.ac.uk
Web: www.sgul.ac.uk

Sheffield

The Medical School
University of Sheffield
Beech Hill Road
Sheffield S10 2RX
Tel: 0114 222 5533
Email: medadmissions@sheffield.ac.uk
Web: www.shef.ac.uk/medicine

Southampton

Faculty of Medicine
University of Southampton
Southampton General Hospital
Tremona Road
Southampton SO16 6YD
Tel: 023 8059 4408
Email: ugapply.fm@southampton.ac.uk
Web: www.southampton.ac.uk/medicine

Swansea

College of Medicine
Grove Building
University of Wales Swansea
Singleton Park
Swansea SA2 8PP
Tel: 01792 513400
Email: medicine@swansea.ac.uk
Web: www.swan.ac.uk/medicine

UCL (and Royal Free)
UCL Medical School
University College London
Gower Street
London WC1E 6BT
Tel: 020 7679 0841
Email: medicaladmissions@ucl.ac.uk
Web: www.ucl.ac.uk/medicalschool

Warwick
Warwick Medical School
University of Warwick
Coventry CV4 7AL
Tel: 02476 574 880
Email: wmsinfo@warwick.ac.uk
Web: www2.warwick.ac.uk/fac/med
Note: Warwick is a graduate-entry only university, not A level entry.

Access to Medicine
The College of West Anglia
Tennyson Avenue
King's Lynn PE30 2QW
Tel: 01553 761144
Email: enquiries@col-westanglia.ac.uk
Web: www.cwa.ac.uk/atm-content.html

Studying outside the UK

Royal College of Surgeons in Ireland
123 St Stephen's Green
Dublin 2
Ireland
Tel: +353 1 402 2248
Email: admissions@rcsi.ie
Web: www.rcsi.ie

Saint George's University School of Medicine
University Centre
Grenada
West Indies
Tel: 0800 169 9061 ext. 9 1380 (from the UK)
Web: www.sgu.edu

Volunteering

Positive East
(HIV/AIDS volunteering)
159 Mile End Road
London E1 4AQ
Tel: 020 7791 2855
Email: volunteering@positiveeast.org.uk
Web: www.positiveeast.org.uk

Tables

Table 10: Medical school admissions policies for 2013–14 entry

Institution	Usual offer	Usual AS requirements	Usual A2 requirements	Retakes considered
Aberdeen	AAA	None	Chemistry + 1 other science/ Maths	In very extenuating circumstances
Barts and The London	AAAa	B in 4th AS and B in either Chemistry or Biology AS	Two must be sciences, either Biology or Chemistry	Only modular resits within 2-year periods acceptable
Birmingham	AAA– A*AA	A in Biology	Chemistry + 1 other science/ Maths	In extenuating circumstances and if narrowly missed AAA
Brighton and Sussex	AAA or A*AB	Both Biology and Chemistry to A grade	Biology + Chemistry at A grades	In extenuating circumstances and if narrowly missed AAA
Bristol	AAA– A*AB	Fourth AS at grade C+	Chemistry at A grade + 1 other lab-based science (one of Human Biology, Biology or Physics)	Accepts AS module resits but not A2 level retakes
Cambridge	A*AA	3rd science/ Maths	Chemistry + 2 other science/ Maths	In extenuating circumstances
Cardiff	AAA	Biology + Chemistry; A in Biology/ Chemistry if not at A2	Biology/ Chemistry	If previously applied to Cardiff
Dundee	AAA	Biology	Chemistry + 1 other science/ Maths	Does not consider applications based on retaken examinations
Durham	AAA	If only one of Biology and Chemistry at AS/A2, other at GCSE	Biology/ Chemistry	In extenuating circumstances
East Anglia A100	AAAb	B in 4th AS	Biology	Yes (BBB from first sitting)
East Anglia A104	BCC	No AS requirement	No usual requirements	Resits not accepted

Table 10: Continued

Institution	Usual offer	Usual AS requirements	Usual A2 requirements	Retakes considered
Edinburgh	AAAb	Biology; B in 4th AS	Chemistry + 1 other science/ Maths + B in GCSE English	In extenuating circumstances (evidence must be verified prior to UCAS application)
Glasgow[1]	AAA	Biology	Chemistry + 1 other science/ Maths + B in GCSE English	Resits for any qualification not considered
Hull York	AAA– AAB	B in 4th AS	Biology + Chemistry at grade As	In extenuating circumstances
Imperial	AAAb or AAAC	B in 4th AS or C in 4th A2	Biology/ Chemistry	In extenuating circumstances and if previously applied to Imperial (CCC at first sitting and AAA in winter examinations and it is mentioned in referee's statement)
Keele	AAAb– A*ABb	B in 4thAS	Biology/ Chemistry	No
King's	AAAb/ AAAC/ AAaab	Biology + Chemistry; grade B	Biology/ Chemistry	In extenuating circumstances
Leeds	AAA	None	Chemistry at grade A	In extenuating circumstances
Leicester	AAA	Biology	Chemistry	In extenuating circumstances and if previously held Leicester offer
Liverpool	AAAb	B in 4th subject	Biology + Chemistry + 3rd + 4th AS	In extenuating circumstances (minimum CCC at first attempt)
Manchester	AAA	4 AS subjects excluding General Studies	Chemistry + 1 other science	In extenuating circumstances and if narrowly missed AAA

Table 10: Continued

Institution	Usual offer	Usual AS requirements	Usual A2 requirements	Retakes considered
Newcastle	AAA	If only 1 of Biology and Chemistry at AS/A2, other at GCSE	Biology/ Chemistry	In extenuating circumstances with supporting evidence from GP or school
Nottingham	AAA	AA in Biology + Chemistry; 6 GCSEs at A+	Biology + Chemistry at grade As	In extenuating circumstances
Oxford[2]	AAA	Not specified	Chemistry + Biology and/or Physics and/or Maths	See advice on website
Peninsula	A*AA– AAAb	B in 4th AS	Chemistry + Biology/Physics	Yes (AAB at first attempt then A*AA/AAA)
Queen's Belfast	AAA	At least a grade B in AS Biology/ Human Biology	Chemistry + Biology/Physics	If previously held Queen's offer and missed by 1 grade (AABa at first attempt)
St Andrews	AAA	GCSE Biology + Maths if not AS/A2	Chemistry + 1 other science/ Maths	In extenuating circumstances
St George's	AAA	Biology + Chemistry B in 4th AS	Biology/ Chemistry	No
Sheffield	AAA	Chemistry + other science	AAA in Chem- istry + other science	No
Southampton	AAA	B in Chemistry/ Biology	Biology/Chem- istry	In extenuating circumstances and if retaking one subject
UCL	AAA	4th subject Chemistry + Biology	Chemistry	Not recommended to apply

[1] Retake candidates will normally be expected to achieve AAA.
[2] Oxford offers two courses:

- A100: a six-year course in medicine (graduates may apply and complete this course in five years). Contact address: Administrative Officer, Medical Sciences Teaching Centre, South Parks Road, Oxford OX1 3PL; tel: 01865 285783; email: admissions@medschool.ox.ac.uk

- A101: a four-year accelerated course (for graduates in experimental sciences). Contact address: Medical Sciences Office, John Radcliffe Hospital, Headington, Oxford OX3 9DU; tel: 01865 228975; email: Lesley.maitland@medsci.ox.ac.uk

Note: Details were correct when going to press – check websites for updated information.

Table 11: Medical school interview and written test policies for 2012 entry

Institution	Typical length (minutes)	Number on the panel	Test
Aberdeen	17–18	2	UKCAT
Birmingham	15	3	UKCAT
Brighton and Sussex	20	3	UKCAT
Barts and The London	15–20	2–3	UKCAT
Bristol	15–20	2	None
Cambridge	2 × 20–30	2–3	BMAT
Cardiff	20	2–3	UKCAT
Dundee	MMI: 10 stations × 7	–	UKCAT
Durham	45	2	UKCAT
East Anglia	MMI: 7 stations × 6	–	UKCAT: case history discussion
Edinburgh	Undergraduates not normally interviewed	–	UKCAT
Glasgow	15–20	2	UKCAT
Hull York	20	2	UKCAT
Imperial	15 for undergraduate	3–4	BMAT
	15 for postgraduate	3–4	UKCAT
Keele	20 (varies – may be standard or MMI)	3	UKCAT
King's	15–30	2	UKCAT
Leeds	20 (varies – may be standard or MMI)	3	UKCAT
Leicester	20	2	UKCAT
Liverpool	15	2	None
Manchester	MMI (2 hours)	3	UKCAT
Newcastle	30	2	UKCAT
Nottingham	15	2	UKCAT
Oxford	2 × 20–30	2–4	BMAT
Peninsula	20	2–3	UKCAT
Queen's Belfast	MMI: 9 stations × 5	–	UKCAT
St Andrews	20	2–3	UKCAT
St George's	MMI: 7 stations × 5	4	UKCAT
Sheffield	20	2–3	UKCAT

Table 11: Continued

Institution	Typical length (minutes)	Number on the panel	Test
Southampton	School leavers and graduates not normally interviewed unless further information is required to consider application (only international students)	2	UKCAT
UCL	15–20	3	BMAT

MMIs are multi mini interviews, a series of small interviews or tasks the candidate has to complete. Their content varies with the medical school that carries them out. See the individual websites for more details.

Source: ISC Medical (www.medical-interviews.co.uk/).

Glossary of terms

AIDS (acquired immune deficiency syndrome)
AIDS is a disease that affects the immune system, lowering the body's resistance to infection. The disease is caused by the human immuno-deficiency virus (HIV).

BMA (British Medical Association)
The professional medical association and trade union for doctors and medical students.

BMAT (BioMedical Admissions Test)
An admissions test required by certain universities. See page 33 for a list of universities that require this test.

BMI (body mass index)
Indicates whether someone is overweight or underweight, based on their weight and height.

GAMSAT (Graduate Australian Medical School Admissions Test)
A test introduced in 1999 by some universities to aid in the selection of candidates who already have degrees.

GEP (Graduate Entry Programme)
A four-year programme offered by universities for students who already have a degree, as opposed to the traditional five-year programme.

GMC (General Medical Council)
The governing body that protects, promotes and maintains the health and safety of the public by ensuring proper standards in the practice of medicine.

H5N1
An influenza subtype, also known as avian flu or 'bird flu'.

Integrated courses
Those where basic medical sciences are taught concurrently with clinical studies. Thus, this style is a compromise between a traditional course and a PBL course.

Intercalated degree
An intercalated degree is a one-year course of study after the pre-clinical years to attain a further degree, e.g. in biochemistry or anatomy.

MB (Bachelor of Medicine)
One of the three degrees that can be awarded by medical schools to students after four or five years of academic study.

MBBS (Bachelor of Medicine and Surgery)
One of the three degrees that can be awarded by medical schools to students after four or five years of academic study.

MBChB
Some medical schools award this degree instead of the MBBS. This depends on the medical school.

MMC (Modernising Medical Careers)
An association within the NHS that provides doctors with information on specialist training.

MMR (measles, mumps and rubella)
A vaccination given to young children around the age of one.

MRI (magnetic resonance imaging)
A medical imaging technique used in radiology to visualise detailed internal structures of the body.

MRSA (methicillin-resistant *Staphylococcus aureus*)
A bacterium responsible for several difficult-to-treat infections in humans. It is also called multidrug-resistant bacteria.

NICE (National Institute for Health and Clinical Excellence)
NICE sets standards for quality healthcare and produces guidance on medicines, treatments and procedures.

PBL (problem-based learning)
The medical training that some medical schools use and is a more patient-oriented approach than the more traditional lecture styles.

Personal statement
The written document provided by the candidate about themselves which is sent with the university application to the medical schools.

SARS (severe acute respiratory syndrome)
A very serious form of pneumonia which saw an outbreak in 2002 and 2003.

Student BMJ
A publication produced for prospective medical students.

Traditional courses
Longer established and following a lecture-based style, using didactic methods. The majority of these courses are subject-based ones, where lectures are the most appropriate way of delivering the information.

UCAS (Universities and Colleges Admissions Service)
The association that all applications to university go through when applying to medical school or any higher education college.

UCAS codes
The identifying letters and numbers of the various university courses. These are vital when making your application. Medical courses range from A100 to A104 depending on previous experience (e.g. A levels, degree, etc.).

UKCAT (United Kingdom Clinical Aptitude Test)
An application test that certain medical schools require students to sit before accepting them onto the course. See page 28 for clarification of which universities require this test.

WHO (World Health Organization)
A specialised agency of the United Nations that acts as a coordinating authority on international public health.

Work experience
Voluntary work (normally) organised before you apply to medical school which is described in your personal statement. This is a vital component of your application.

Postscript

If you have any comments or questions arising from this book, the staff of MPW and I would be very happy to answer them. You can contact us at the address given below. Good luck with your application to medical school!

Simon Horner

MPW (London)
90/92 Queen's Gate
London SW7 5AB
Tel: 020 7835 1355
Fax: 020 7259 2705
Email: enquiries@mpw.co.uk